UNLEASHING
THE POWER WITHIN

HOW TO CHANGE WHO YOU ARE
TO GET WHAT YOU WANT

UNLEASHING THE POWER WITHIN

HOW TO CHANGE WHO YOU ARE TO GET WHAT YOU WANT

Joe Land

1stBooks – rev. 9/19/00

Dedicated with love to Krista.
My pal, partner, and happiness teacher.

ACKNOWLEDGMENTS

To tell you the truth I've never written a book before, but the folks who know about such things tell me that it's appropriate for an author to acknowledge everyone who had a part in the creation and publishing of a book. So, here goes.

First on the list would have to be my agent, Julie Parham. Julie apparently earns her living by going all over the country saying, "You know, you ought to write a book," to everyone she meets. And I happen to be one of the poor souls who took her seriously, without having any idea what I was letting myself in for. To hear Julie tell it, because I already had what I wanted to say organized for my seminars, the book would virtually write itself. Boy was I dumb to believe that!

But even if she *didn't* fully believe that, I realize now that she knew that if she could just prod me into beginning the book, I would get hooked and eventually produce something that I would be proud of for the rest of my life. The truth is, I can't give her enough credit. She envisioned this book long before I did. In fact she had to sell it twice. First to me, then to the publisher. And then she stood toe to toe at different times with both of us when we got off track from what she had known from the beginning it could be.

Now that it's over, I can tell you honestly that I will be forever grateful to Julie for having the vision, the insight, and the ability to make it all happen. But I also have to tell you that should you ever meet Julie Parham, when she says those tempting first words to you...run the other way as hard as you can!

When I first began this project, I hired Adam Robinson, who is a very successful author in his own right, as a collaborator. His initial job, at least the way I understood it, was to hold my hand and help me write the book. But, instead, Adam taught *me* how to write it. You see, I have been a public speaker for years and because of my background and lack of formal education I've always addressed my audiences in a kind of home-spun, country

vii

way. Adam was obsessed with the idea that I could have that same "voice" in my writing. I knew he was wrong, but I played along with the idea long enough for him to teach me to write in the exact same tone I speak in. And once he did, he abandoned me to write the book on my own. And so it's Adam who's responsible for you reading the same Joe Land that audiences have always listened to. I'll leave you to decide whether or not that was a good idea, but I will say this; if this book conveys what I have to say in an easy to understand manner, then Adam deserves the credit.

I've always known that every author was assigned an "editor" at the publishing company. But, I have to confess I had no idea what an editor did. Well I found out. As close as I can tell, an editor is a cross between an English teacher and a mother. They assigned me to Elizabeth Zack, a real taskmaster. It was her job to wait until I thought I had finished the manuscript and then load it down with hundreds of little sticky notes and send it back to me. These "flags" as she calls them, might say something as mild as, "This wording is a little awkward, can you fix?", to things that even she felt the need to apologize for like, "Let's try a new intro for this piece, this start up seems a bit too—dull (sorry)". Of course after a few of those, I would decide that she couldn't be pleased and I just wasn't going to be able to write this book. But at precisely that point each time she would throw in a little note that said something like, "Excellent—what a wonderful story!" (That's where the mother part comes in.) And like a little kid, I would be so proud that I would hit it again with a new determination and enthusiasm for making the book as good as I could.

The thing that really irked me about working with Elizabeth was that no matter how hard I tried and how good the next chapter I sent her would be, she always seemed to find a way...to make it better. But she wasn't so hot. I don't think she made the book more than three times better than it would have been without her. So here's to Elizabeth Zack, who managed to get more out of me than either of us thought I was capable of.

Back when I was still in business, Jobi Hill served as my assistant for seven or eight years before she decided to take a sabbatical and start her family. She was the ultimate answer to the fact that I can't type (they don't teach typing by the eighth grade), that I can't remember where I'm supposed to go, or what I said at the last place I went. She was probably the highest paid executive assistant in town simply because I couldn't live without her. When I started this book, I begged and pleaded with her to come back long enough to help me get it done. So we wrote the book with me on the road, in between prison seminars, FEDEXing dictation tapes, and faxing edited manuscripts back and forth until we finally got it done. Jobi (or mommy, as she now prefers to be called) has informed me by telephone that she has pulled most of her hair out over this book and is going back to her life. She then added that I should not try to come after her. She's the only one who could have put up with me through this work and I will always be thankful that she hung in there and typed every word of this thing while watching Samantha out of the corner of her eye and holding T.J. on her lap. Thank you, Jobi! *(You're welcome, Joe—but don't ever ask me to do it again!)*.

There is one more person that I must extend a special acknowledgment to, my old friend, Ed Foreman. Ed is the only man in this century to have served in the United States Congress from two states, Texas and New Mexico. When he got out of politics we all thought he might go straight and begin earning an honest living but, unfortunately, he turned to public speaking instead. Ed is also the only friend I have who shares with me the dubious honor of being featured on CBS News' 60 Minutes.

In a way, Ed didn't have anything at all to do with this book. But, in another way, he had *everything* to do with it. Although I've been influenced by a lot of people, if I had to name one mentor it would be Ed Foreman. He single-handedly taught me a couple of the life's lessons in this book. He was the first one to ever point out to me the possibility that I "can have a *good* day, *all* day, *every* day." But he taught me something else just as valuable. He showed me that people are hungry for that message. And he convinced me with his seminar audiences that people would take it and use it to make their lives better. In short, he's taught me a lot of what's in this book and his accomplishments have motivated me to write it.

I'm honestly glad I had a chance to acknowledge all of these folks because between them they had more to do with this book than I did. And I'm genuinely thankful that each of them came into my life and made their unique contribution.

TABLE OF CONTENTS

PART THREE:
MASTERING YOUR MIND
BY MANAGING YOUR THOUGHTS

Introduction

The Road From Self-Defeat
to Self-Mastery and the
Lessons Along the Way

Welcome!

By picking up this book, you've taken the first step in an exciting journey, one that we'll be taking together. I've presented the information you're about to read to thousands of people around the country in live speeches and seminars, but, for the next couple of hundred or so pages, you and I will be having a private discussion.

I'm going to let you in on the secrets I wish someone had shared with me, things I had to learn the hard way—insights that can change the course of your entire life.

Just a Guy Named Joe

But before I begin showing you how to gain control of the enormous power you have deep within you, let's take a few moments and get acquainted. With just a little of my personal history you'll better understand how and why I formulated the unique Life Lessons you're about to learn.

Although my dad worked in the oil fields and we moved around a lot, I grew up mostly in the small farming community of Dimmitt, Texas. I must tell you up front that I'm not at all proud of my childhood. I spent my teenage years in a constant state of rebellion against everything and everyone that represented authority. It seemed I was always in trouble, taking another of those familiar trips down to the principal's office or flunking yet another class. In fact, I was such a terrible student that midway through my second attempt at the ninth grade I gave up and left school for good.

And I'm afraid things didn't improve much in the adult world when I got there either. Oh, I wasn't a bad kid, but I did have a terrible attitude. And as a result, I wasn't very productive. I couldn't even hold down a job because I couldn't force myself to get up early enough to go to work on time. And so, after about a year of bouncing from job to job, my self-esteem getting lower with each new failure, I decided, at seventeen, to join the Navy.

The military didn't require a high school diploma back then, and so, after somehow making it through boot camp, I found myself working on the flight deck of an aircraft carrier. Boy, was this new job different from my old ones. My new employers *insisted* I come to work on time. They also made it clear that I would shape up quickly or face the consequences.

Well, I'm sure you won't be surprised to hear that it wasn't long before I found myself in the ship's brig—standing at rigid attention staring at the shiniest cell door you can imagine—while outside stood the world's ugliest Marine. His primary pur-pose in life, it turned out, was to watch me and make life miserable for me if I did anything wrong, like glance at him for an instant instead of staring straight ahead.

And as strange as it may sound, that was one of the best days of my life! Oh, I admit it didn't seem like a very good day at the time. In fact, I thought it was the worst, but as I look back I can see that it was a major turning point. As I stood behind that cell door, scared and depressed, I realized my life was a real mess.

But somehow I was smart enough to figure out who was responsible for the mess. I realized that my attitude toward life and my bad habits were my own worst enemies.

That day I made what was, up until that point at least, the biggest decision of my life. I decided—at the ripe old age of seventeen—that from that moment forward things would have to change. But I realized the only way I could make my life better was to change who and what I was. I had an idea how tough this would be, but I so desperately needed to feel good about myself that I became determined to do whatever it took to become a person I could have some good feelings about.

Searching for Success

I suppose you could say that day marked the start of my study of self-mastery. And since then I've devoted my life to learning how to change, to stop being the old Joe Land and to transform myself into a person I'd rather be.

The first lesson I learned in those early years was that the key to change was desire. Only after I became convinced that I really *wanted* to change did I find a way to begin the process in earnest. And each time my desire to continue the transformation would begin to diminish and I'd begin slipping back into my old habits and attitudes, I would bolster my desire by intensely visualizing the person I wanted to become. I'd see myself having the things that kind of person could acquire and living the lifestyle they live. And as I allowed myself to dream of being the person I hoped I could be, the resulting desire would make me strong again, and I would once again find the power to bring more and more of my life under control.

Little by little, things did get better. I received an honorable discharge from the Navy at twenty-one (a feat that in itself shocked most of the people who had known me very long) and I thought I was ready for the world!

I felt the need at that point for a specific goal to aim for. I knew if I didn't have a dream I wouldn't be able to keep my thoughts focused in a positive way. So, I decided to make money my goal. I vowed to become a multimillionaire by the time I was thirty-five. I figured that I needed a way of measuring the success of my transformation—and what better way to calculate success than money? But, like anyone who pursues a goal without moderation, I would become so focused on wealth that I would go overboard. Back then I was convinced that life was a game and you kept score in dollars and cents.

So there I was, fresh out of the Navy, armed with nothing but a dream of becoming fabulously wealthy and a consuming desire to find a way to make that dream a reality. And when I say the dream was all I had, that's exactly what I mean. I had no money, no credit, no education...shoot, I didn't even *know*

xv

anybody who had enough money to pay more than that week's bills.

It was a cinch that my lack of education was going to keep me from getting a very good job, and besides, I knew I couldn't become wealthy working for someone else. So in my early twenties I became an entrepreneur. My first business was a four-for-a-dollar hamburger stand. The fellow I bought it from had earned such a terrible reputation with his bankers that they were desperate enough to get him off of their books to allow me to take his place. And so after signing my life away, this uneducated dreamer put on an apron and started flipping hamburger patties.

But when faced with the task of parlaying that humble beginning into the riches I wanted, I found I still had a major problem. In fact, it was more than just a problem-it was an enemy. As determined as I was to realize my goals, this enemy was equally determined that I should never realize them. He was always there, constantly shadowing me everywhere I went. No matter how hard I tried to escape him, he kept inventing ways to pull me away from my dreams of wealth and make me do a lot of counterproductive (and stupid) things.

And that person—my enemy—was Joe Land.

My Own Worst Enemy

Two things kept me from reaching my goal in those early days of my entrepreneurial career. First, I couldn't seem to get myself to do all the things I knew I needed to do on a consistent basis, day after day, in order to realize my dreams. (That was because most of them weren't much fun to do.) And second, to make matters even worse, I couldn't *keep* myself from doing a lot of counterproductive things, because they *were* fun.

So early on I learned that my emotions and feelings made wonderful servants but terrible masters. I *had* to become a person who was capable of doing a number of things that I didn't particularly feel like doing, and at the same time I needed to be able to keep myself from doing things that I enjoyed but that would rob me of my success. I had to find a way to gain better control of that one person who could help me immensely but who appeared to be dedicated to my failure: me.

If I was going to be successful in any area of my life, I had to have a special kind of power, a power that most people don't have.

I came to call it "The Ultimate Power", and it's the only kind of power I've ever needed in order to achieve or to become anything I ever set my mind to. In fact, I've become convinced it's the only kind of power anyone ever needs. The ultimate power is power over myself.

So, I busied myself gaining a deeper understanding of how my mind works and why I did the things I did. And slowly but surely I began to formulate and develop some simple but powerful techniques that gave me a larger degree of control over my emotions and feelings.

Then, I made one of the most important discoveries of my life. I learned that it wasn't necessary for me to go find the ultimate power...because I already possessed it! All of my failures and lack of self-control hadn't resulted from not having the ultimate power; they occurred because I didn't *know* I had it. I came to understand that each of us has all of the power he or she will ever need—the power to have, do, or be anything we want. And once I learned that the solution to all of my problems was within me, I began to focus on the process of learning to harness this elusive power, so I could put it to work for me instead of allowing it to continue to defeat me. The knowledge that resulted from this study allowed me to radically change my behavior into the kind of action I knew was necessary to reach my goals.

After making a minor success out of my hamburger stand and then starting and running several other small and mildly successful business ventures, I decided to try real estate. I began as a salesman, then became a broker, and finally started my own real estate brokerage firm. I also began investing in real estate and, fortunately, by the late seventies the real estate market became a very lucrative place to be.

Along the way I learned some very innovative techniques for buying real estate. After a while I decided to start sharing these secrets with others. So I started offering real estate seminars— lots of them. In fact, eventually hundreds of thousands of people attended those courses. I was rolling by then, my professional life just getting better and better.

Although I missed my goal of becoming a multimillionaire by age thirty-five, I was only a few years late. In my early forties I was making big money—as much as four or five hundred thousand dollars a year. Then, to top it off, in 1988, I shocked myself and everyone who'd ever known me by making ten million dollars in that single twelve-month period!

I was thrilled. My dreams had come true in spades. I had made it!

But, in a very strange way, that year turned out to be yet another watershed for me—as life-changing as the one that occurred in that ship's brig when I was seventeen.

You see, I had enough money at that point to have the life I had envisioned all those years. After all, I could buy anything I wanted. I could go anywhere, do anything. Yet something was wrong.

Financial Success Is Not Enough

One day it became obvious that I was going to have to sit down and get very honest with myself and try to figure out what the problem was.

I must admit to you that while I was extraordinarily successful from a financial standpoint, the rest of my life was a disaster area. As a husband and father, I was a failure, a workaholic whose life was totally consumed with making money. I was so involved in what I wanted, I couldn't see that my selfishness was keeping me from being a whole person. But even coming face-to-face with these failures didn't seem to go all the way to the root of the problem.

So I explored my feelings further by asking myself what the money *hadn't* done for me. And then I had to—as silly as it sounds—admit to myself that all that money hadn't made me happy.

Now, I know what you're thinking. "Doesn't sound like a problem to me! Give *me* the ten million dollars and I'll show you how to be happy." Is that close? Well, my friend, I used to feel the very same way. But stop and think a minute. I'm sure you know of someone who is miserable despite having great wealth. And I'm sure you also know some grandmother-type who's always had to scrimp and save and has trouble getting in and out of her rocking chair, yet who seems blissfully happy.

I had to face the fact that I had only learned how to make money—I still didn't know how to live life. Oh, as long as I was in hot pursuit of the money, climbing the hill, I was inspired and motivated by the anticipation of everything being wonderful just as soon as I became fabulously wealthy. But when more money fell on me than I ever dreamed possible, the reality of the fulfillment of that dream was truly life altering. When you stand at the top of the mountain, having no further to climb, and the reward you've thought about all during the climb isn't there, it does major things to the way you think.

So, after a period of introspection, I finally admitted to myself that the money, the one commodity I had dedicated my entire life to, had not given me what I thought it would. And to make matters even worse, I hadn't even known what that was supposed to be!

Searching for Happiness

I realized, then, that money was never really my goal, but the means to reach a goal. The real goal I had always pursued without even realizing it was happiness.

At that point in my life I sold all of my companies, retired from business, and secluded myself in order to take on a completely new project. The new goal was simple: Find out exactly what happiness is and the most efficient way to attain a maximum amount of the stuff.

So I studied happiness. I studied everyone I could find who had anything to say on the subject. The great philosophers. The psychologists. The theologians. But most of all, I began to observe people who appeared to be genuinely happy...and I found out some very interesting things.

Among the books I read during that period was *In Search of Identity: The Autobiography of Anwar Sadat.* Most people don't know that Sadat spent a year in prison awaiting trial for a crime he was later exonerated of. This year was spent not only in prison but in solitary confinement. And this great man, who would go on to be the president of his country and revered around the world as one of the ultimate peacemakers of all times, said that the happiest time of his life was the last eight months he spent in that dreary, dingy, tiny prison cell with a bunk, a toilet, and four walls. I couldn't believe my eyes. Once I satisfied myself that I had, indeed, read the passage correctly and there wasn't some typographical error, I read on to find out how such an outlandish statement could be true.

Sadat said most of us make the mistake of looking for happiness outside us, in circumstances or possessions. But he said he was fortunate enough to be put in a situation where his happiness clearly could not come from his environment. His only alternative was to look inward, where he discovered the key to happiness.

At that point I realized, for the first time in my life, what happiness is. Happiness is a *state of mind*! The elusive goal we all strive so hard for can only occur between our left ear and our right ear. Why, then, are we so busy looking for it outside us? Do we really think we're going to arrange the situations and circumstances of our life in such a way as to somehow magically achieve that state of mind?

It doesn't work that way. Now I realize why the ten million dollars didn't make me happy. Happiness is not an external concept you go find. Nothing can *make* you happy. *You* must make *yourself* happy. Happiness is an internal state of mind that everyone is responsible for creating for him or herself.

It was then that I realized that the power that waits inside us to be tapped was much more than merely the ability to control our behavior in certain areas of our lives. The true definition of "the ultimate power", I decided, was *gaining control of your emotions, your feelings, your thoughts, your moods, and your attitudes so that if you desire a particular state of mind, like happiness, you'll have the ability to take control of the inner workings of your being and create that state for yourself.* That's the ultimate power! And once you realize you have this power and learn to use it, you can make dramatic changes in your life.

Why You Need the Ultimate Power

Most people think that to succeed in life, they need to have power over other people and other things. Nothing could be further from the truth.

You are the only person you really have an opportunity to control. I think that, morally, you're the only person you really should attempt to control. And probably you are also the toughest person to control. Most of us don't understand enough about ourselves to even try.

I can tell you from experience that the only power you'll ever need to reach success in whatever area you want is the power over you. Do you want more money? You'll need better control over yourself! Do you want to become a better person? You'll need the power to change! Do you want greater happiness? You'll need to find and use your power within!

The ultimate power, the power you have within you, will help you to get yourself to do those things that cause you some discomfort for the moment but that you know are good for you in the long run. It's the power to get yourself to stop doing those things that you like to do—the things that are gratifying to do right now—but are damaging to the goals you've set for yourself. In short, it's the power to make your feelings take a backseat to your better judgment.

If you're doing something counterproductive or self-defeating, you must learn how to stop that behavior. If

xxi

something inside you is pulling you away from your goals, or even causing you harm, you need to learn the concepts I'm going to offer you in the following pages. If you're overeating and diminishing your life as a result, or if you're drinking too much, or if you're procrastinating and unable to get yourself to do the things necessary to reach your personal or professional goals, if there's *any* kind of commitment to yourself that you can't keep, then this is your book—read on!

The Two Goals We All Share

As you consider the following pages, there are a couple of principles I'd like for you to keep in mind. I'll explain them both in depth a little later on, but it's best to have a basic understanding of them as you begin your quest to unleash the power within.

The "Lower and Higher" Principle

First, let me give you a little preview of a concept I call lower and higher purposes. I don't know whether you've ever noticed it or not, but we're designed so that as we pursue a lower (selfish) goal or motivation, we automatically accomplish a higher mission.

I'll give you a couple of examples. For the most part, our motivation for eating is that it's pleasurable. The simple fact is that food *tastes* good and there's satisfaction a big, delicious meal gives us what we just can't get any other way. But in pursuing the need to satisfy our personal hunger and enjoying the pleasure of eating, we fuel our body and, in doing so, fulfill the higher mission—the real reason for eating (and, of course, the reason for our *desire* to eat)—providing sustenance for our physical existence...providing fuel for our bodies in order to stay alive.

The act of sex is another example. Other than the married couple who is having trouble conceiving, and are making a diligent effort to carry out a plan their doctor has given them, most people are not thinking about the end result of their love making at the time it happens.

Let's face it, we have sex because it's *fun*. But that isn't the real purpose for the activity...the real mission, of course, is procreation. The ongoing survival of our species. And we carry out that mission inadvertently and automatically.

My point is, the concept of lower and higher purpose is an intricate part of how we're put together. As we pursue out selfish needs—provided we pursue them in the right way—we bring about the accomplishment of a much higher, much more worthy goal or mission.

Happiness Is Your Goal

We are all pursuing the same goal: happiness. This relentless, ongoing pursuit is the single most important and overriding motivation in your life. After all, how do you formulate your goals and dreams? The answer is simple. You make plans to do or become what you think will make you happy. It governs how we choose our relationships—and it's how we select what we want out of life. I submit that the only reason you ever want to be, have, or do anything is because of the happiness you think it will bring you.

And so the first idea I want you to bear in mind as you become involved in learning how to gain control of the tremendous potential that lies within you is that your primary goal in life is to obtain happiness.

Now in case you're thinking that this seems like a terribly shallow reason for living, let me remind you that it's there to serve as the selfish motivation (our reason for doing something) that causes you to attain your real mission in life, your higher goal. Once you truly understand what happiness is, you need not worry about leading a selfish, narcissistic life as a result of pursuing it. You see, like eating or making love, following your selfish need for happiness in the right manner will lead you to the accomplishment of your higher mission.

Life Is a School

But what is our higher mission—the real reason for your presence on this planet? It's to grow, develop, learn, and mature. What else could we be here for? There's nothing else you will take with you when you leave this life. You will only be able to leave here with what you've *become* as a result of the *experience*. Growth is what you're really here for, and the pursuit of real, genuine happiness can *only* be yours as you engage in the continuing achievement of this grand purpose.

You see, this life is really a gigantic school, a training ground of magnificent proportions. What is life all about? It's about having experiences that give you the opportunity to learn and grow. And the need for growth and the attainment of maturity is the secret underlying psychological need that, in each of us, must be met as the primary prerequisite for happiness and fulfillment.

Yes, every experience in your life is nothing more than another lesson in your own personal curriculum in the school we all attend. Each person you've ever met, or will ever meet, is a teacher, able to provide you with yet another valuable piece of your education.

I don't expect you, at this point, to fully comprehend or appreciate the depth or the consequences of understanding these two concepts. But I will show you, later on, the tremendous change that occurs in the life of anyone who alters his or her perception of what's going on here to accommodate the belief that the sole purpose of our physical existence is to provide us with the opportunity to grow and mature, and that we are designed in a way that causes maturity to evolve from our pursuit of happiness.

Once I began to understand these two concepts and how they work together, the lessons in life became much easier to learn and I found that I could benefit from virtually anything that happened. The process of growth is always much easier, and faster, if we help it along. I've now come to view my life as a series of lessons. Some of them—the ones I was exposed to before I understood the process—were learned at great cost.

There were lessons I learned from pain—generally caused by my own mistakes—while other lessons were easy, like a light bulb going on. Then there were magnificent lessons I learned from joyful experiences as I inadvertently stumbled into the right way to live life.

In the book you hold in your hands I've gathered the most important lessons I've learned over the past three decades. It's said that the truly wise person learns from other people's mistakes; the smart person learns from his or her own mistakes; and the fool never learns at all. I hope that you can derive as much benefit from my mistakes and the lessons I learned from them as I have. Within these pages you'll find magnificent secrets...secrets that will allow you to have, do, or be virtually anything you want. But most important, you'll discover the principles that will allow you to lead a rich, full, complete life...to truly live instead of just existing. Soon it will be evident to you that to fulfill your fondest dreams you only have to overcome yourself. And I'm going to show you how to do exactly that.

Are you ready to gain the knowledge that will allow you to begin unleashing the power you have within? Great! Let's get started!

PART ONE

The Battle Within

Life Lesson 1

Your Strongest, Most Determined Adversary is....You

What Do You Want Out of Life?

Sadly, the vast majority of people simply exist. Oh, most folks find a way to get by day to day, exerting themselves just enough to stay within the boundaries of what is acceptable, but they never really have any idea of what true enrichment and fulfillment can be.

I truly believe that you and I are here to enjoy this life, to live it as an adventure, and gain from it all we possibly can. What would you like to accomplish? What would you like to achieve in material terms? What are your self-improvement goals? What sorts of relationships would you like to have? What kind of person would you like to be?

Well, let me tell you that there's only one major obstacle keeping you from reaching these goals. And guess what? The obstacle is...you! You are, for the most part, the creator of the circumstances of your life. You've brought them about with your actions, or lack of them.

The accomplishment of anything is a two-step process. First, you must learn *how* to achieve whatever it is you want. That's the easy part. You can quickly find out how to do just about anything you'd ever want to do.

If you want to become a brain surgeon, for instance, all you have to do is get face-to-face with someone who has become one and in five minutes you'll know the exact steps to take. The surgeon will tell you the prerequisites for medical school, the best schools to attend, how long it will take, the subjects you'll have to study, and so on. Knowing what to do is the easy part.

But the second step, getting yourself to *do* those things you learned in step one, is another matter altogether. Most of us are capable of about any accomplishment—but can we get ourselves

3

to go do it? Sadly, most of us run into a great deal of internal resistance when we try to live up to even the smallest of the commitments we've made to ourselves.

So, we must begin our search for the power to change by admitting to ourselves, once and for all, that *we* are our toughest adversary. After all, who else could it be? Who else has the time to stay with you twenty four hours a day and continually keep you from doing the things that you're otherwise capable of, and from having the things you could have as a result?

As I go around the country presenting my concepts in speeches and seminars, I always begin by asking the audience a few questions. These questions are designed to illustrate exactly what the ultimate power is. I ask them to raise their hands and leave them up if they can answer yes to any one of my questions. I tell them that my goal is to get every hand in the room up in the air.

The questions are pretty simple. Here's the first: "How many of you here would like to lose some weight?" Slowly at first—some people are shy—but sure enough, about three-fourths of the hands in the room eventually go up.

It doesn't take me long to get the rest of them up, either. I ask the second question: "How many of you would like to quit smoking?" Some of the hands already raised go up even higher, and, of course, some new ones go up. "How many of you would like to stop procrastinating so you can get more done toward accomplishing your goals?" A lot more hands. Almost everyone in the room has his or her hand up by now.

Then I ask: "Who would like to gain better control over your emotions, the ones that sometimes take over and cause you to do things you later regret? Emotions like fear, anger, jealousy, or resentment?"

As you can imagine, by that time I've accomplished my goal: Every person in the room has at least one hand in the air. And those people all get knowing looks on their faces when I remind them that the one thing all those questions had in common was that they were all about things that they—and only they—are in total control of.

4

You Are in Control of the Most Important
Factor in Your Success

We all realize this, don't we? Our success and satisfaction in life are not determined by our upbringing or our past or even our present circumstances. Although these factors do, of course, influence us to varying degrees, deep down we know the only person responsible for what we get out of life is ourselves.

Which of those questions would you have responded to? Would you, for instance, have joined the majority in every audience who tell me they feel the need to take off some excess pounds? There's a 75 percent chance your answer is yes.

Well, what if I came back next year and asked you the same question; do you think I'd get the same response? The likelihood is that a year from now your desire to lose weight won't have changed. In fact, there's a good chance you'll have some additional pounds you'd like to take off by then!

Now let's think about that for a moment. If you want to lose weight, why don't you just do it? We all know how to take off those extra pounds—it's simple. Eat less and exercise more. After all, who's in charge of what goes in your mouth? When was the last time somebody broke into your house in the middle of the night, got into your refrigerator, and woke you up by cramming a bunch of food in your face?

You are in charge of how much you eat. Or whether or not you smoke. Or whether or not you procrastinate. And believe it or not, you're also in charge of what emotions you feel. You're certainly in charge of how you're *affected* by those emotions and whether or not they take control of your actions.

How many times have your emotional needs for pleasure and relaxation caused you to procrastinate instead of working toward the accomplishment of something that is important to you? How many times have we each looked back and clearly seen that we took the wrong course of action because our emotions steered us in the wrong direction? Then there's our fear of failure, which stops us from venturing out into unknown territory—something that's absolutely necessary if we're going to do new things and try to become something that we've never been.

Years ago, when I was teaching real estate investment seminars, I couldn't help but notice something really strange that happened again and again.

I was teaching a set of exotic and very exciting real estate acquisition techniques. It was a very sophisticated method of buying real estate without having to use any of your own cash. And it solved all of the problems that normally accompany a cashless transaction. You could start your ownership of the property with an equity position that you didn't have to pay for. Because of this built-in equity, the property wasn't over financed and would produce a cash flow. It honestly was a tremendous way to make money. In fact, it was one of the very few ways I knew of to make money without having a lot of cash to begin with.

And make no mistake, as I stood before those seminar audiences I explained my techniques so clearly and enthusiastically that everybody in the room got genuinely excited about them. By the time we were through with the course, everybody was convinced that this was their answer! Finally, they'd found a way to break out of the pack and achieve the financial independence they'd always dreamed of. When the seminar was over they virtually floated out of that room, bound and determined that this time was *the* time.

And do you know what those people did with the ideas they were so on fire with? Nothing. Well, that isn't quite true. About 3 to 5 percent of my real estate seminar attendees used the ideas they'd learned and made money. In fact, many of them become quite wealthy. But the other 95 percent...what happened to them? They understood the ideas just as well and they were every bit as enthusiastic as the ones who did find a way to implement the plan. Was it that the ideas and concepts I taught them wouldn't really work? No. They worked for some; they would have worked for all. Was it that people tried to implement the plan and failed? No. That wasn't it either.

6

The simple fact of the matter is that 95 percent of all those millions of Americans who attended real estate investment seminars in the late seventies and early eighties never even attempted to buy one piece of property! They couldn't work up the nerve to present the first offer. They never found a way to gain the confidence necessary to step out into new territory and become real estate investors. Their fear of failure defeated them before they even had a chance to get started.

But desire and fear are not the only tools we use to defeat ourselves. Our pride—I prefer to call it our sense of self-importance—is one of the strongest and most effective enemies we face. While I'm talking about real estate, let me tell you something that happened to me years ago that is a great illustration of how our sense of self-importance gets in our way by trying to get us to make illogical decisions.

A number of years ago I owned a little set of apartments, and for the most part they stayed rented and gave me all the benefits I'd planned on having when I bought them.

But every now and then I would inadvertently lease an apartment to what landlords often refer to as a renter from hell. These are the folks that not only don't pay their rent, they know enough about the law that they don't move out either! You see, if you're a deadbeat and have been thrown out of enough apartments, you slowly begin to become familiar with the law that governs landlords and tenants. And in some states, if a delinquent renter makes all the right legal moves at just the right times, he can drag out his eviction for weeks or even months. In the meanwhile, he's living in the apartment—no one can get him out—rent free, until the process of eviction, with all its mandatory written notices and judicial folderol, is complete.

Well, on this occasion, I had one of these guys in one of my apartments. He hadn't paid his rent and he not only hadn't moved, he wasn't going to—it was obvious he was playing the eviction game.

One day I was complaining about this tenant to a friend of mine who also owned some rental properties. "This guy's already into me for about three hundred dollars", I said, "and

7

there's no end in sight. I think he's going to drag this thing out until I lose three months' worth of rent. At that point I will have lost six hundred dollars, while he just sits in my apartment, rent free."

My friend said, "I know how you can get him out."

"Well, then, please tell me."

"It's real simple," he returned. And then he looked me in the eye and calmly said, "Why don't you pay him to get out."

"What!" I was shocked at the very idea. "This bum owes *me* three hundred dollars and you're telling me that I ought to *give* him some *more* money so he will move out of my apartment that he's been living in rent free for a month and a half?"

My friend's answer was short and to the point. "Sure, why not?"

"Because it's just not right!"

"Are you sure that's really your reason?" he shot back. "Or is it just that it hurts your pride to let this fellow get some more money from you? You know, Joe, your job is not to be this guy's judge and jury. It's not up to you to make all the world's wrongs right, and it's certainly not to mete out punishment to those who don't treat you well. Get this situation back into perspective. It's in *your* best interest to get that apartment vacated as quickly as possible and rent it to someone else so you can begin collecting money again."

I opened my mouth to really let him have it...but even as I began to form the words, I realized he was right.

Believe me, though, my pride didn't think so. I had to gain a firm grip on that part of me and drag it, kicking and screaming, all the way over to that apartment.

I knocked on the front door and when my deadbeat renter opened it, I had two things in my hand (unfortunately, neither of them was a .45 automatic!). One of them was a one hundred dollar bill and the other, a dated Notification of Intent to Vacate for him to sign.

When I told him I would give him the hundred dollars if he would simply be out of my apartment by the next day, a big, cocky grin came to his face. He couldn't believe his good fortune. And when I saw how amused he was, I must tell you that I almost got sick to my stomach. But I hung in there, realizing that my sense of self-importance, which at that point was really taking a beating, was trying desperately to get me to act against my better judgment. In cold dollars and cents (which is what I owned those apartments for in the first place), this was clearly the smartest, most expedient thing to do.

Well, of course, he took the hundred dollars and I'm glad to say he was gone the next day. I re-rented the unit just a few days later, and so I figure at worst, I was a couple of hundred dollars ahead of the game. Did it hurt to do that? Absolutely. But let me tell you what would have hurt more. Had I given in to my false pride, my need to win—to "show him who's boss"— would have overpowered my better judgment even to the point of making me forget my true objective, my reason for owning those apartments.

How many times have you "cut off your nose to spite your face," claiming, "it's just the principle of the thing," or some other piece of rationalization that is actually an excuse for allowing your emotions to take control of you.

And when you hand off the decision making process to *any* of your emotions, whether its fear, desire, anger or any other feeling that tends to pull you away from your better judgment, you're asking for trouble.

Of course, there are also times that your emotional tendencies operate in complete unison with your better judgment and with what's right. If, for instance, you say, "Golly, I'm hungry," and then realize it's noon and you haven't had lunch yet, then complying with your desire, and eating, is appropriate. Every time what you *want* to do matches your better judgment, you find yourself without an inward adversary, and things move smoothly.

Your Own Worst Enemy
It's when you find yourself operating under the control of something that's *against* your better judgment that you have a

9

problem. When anything other than your better judgment is in control of what you think or say or do, you are engaging in self-defeating behavior. And that's precisely what has to be corrected in order for you to become a person who can act in accordance with the commitments you make to yourself.

A number of things inside you work against your better judgment: anger, fear, hatred, jealousy, pride, resentment, desires, cravings, envy...the list is pretty long.

The truth is, most of us who want to lose weight, or achieve most any other goal for that matter, are helpless to do so because we don't have the ultimate power—self-control, self-mastery. And so a lot of us still smoke or have any number of other unwanted habits we wish we didn't have. We're stifled by our fears and settle for a lot less from life than we could have, because we continually defeat ourselves by making excuses for and giving in to our feelings of inadequacy. Oh, if we could only get ourselves on *our* side!

The Horse Before Any Cart

Whatever your view of success, self-mastery is the horse that has to be put in front of that cart. No matter what you want out of life, the key to attaining it is gaining control of *you*. You must somehow find a way to make a friend out of the adversary that dwells within you.

In fact, let me tell you a little secret. You know this tremendous power that I've been telling you is already inside you? It's the power that is now working *against* you.

You see, your challenge is not to go find additional power outside yourself, and it's certainly not about trying to garner someone else's power for your own use. Instead, like all of us, you face the challenge of getting your army all moving in one direction. The struggle that goes on within you not only keeps you from moving in a single direction toward the accomplishment of your goals, it also robs you of the energy you could be using to make those dreams a reality.

I have no desire to give you a definition of success. No one can define success for your life but you. Once you realize that you really can become anything you wish to be, and decide on exactly what it is you want to accomplish, then, at that point, you will have provided yourself with your own unique definition of success.

But make no mistake, no matter what you choose as the road to your own personal destiny, you probably won't be able to get there unless you can find a way to get all of you on that road. You need to travel it in harmony with yourself.

The Enemy Isn't Really You...It's Only a Part of You

For years I believed that my failures were a result of my lack of self-discipline or desire or determination, or that my attitude wasn't positive enough. In particular, I've waged an ongoing battle with my eating habits over the years. For years I was continually overweight, sometimes by as much as seventy-five pounds. Believe me, dieting is something I know a lot about. I guess I've tried every diet known to mankind—and made up a few of my own. And all those dieting failures illustrate so well the problem we all have with resolutions and our inability to gain enough control over ourselves to live up to them.

I was really good at fooling myself. I would always be saying things like, "I'll start that diet Monday. Well, maybe the first of the month will be better. No, better yet, I'll wait until January first. That's the best time to start a diet; may as well wait until then." And of course, I'd gorge myself in the meantime.

I couldn't understand my constant wavering. I seemed to be continually changing my mind. When I was full and bloated and miserable and ashamed of myself for having overeaten, I would resolve to go on a diet the next morning. "I'm not going to eat for six months. I'm going to lose fifty pounds before I even think about food again."

Well, you know how that promise turned out. By eleven thirty the next morning, I was a different person, one who no

11

longer cared about losing weight. And that was terribly frustrating to me. "I sure wish I weren't so fickle. Why do I change my mind so quickly? What do I *really* want, to be thin or to eat?" Naturally, I had myself a big lunch while I tried to figure out my lack of willpower.

Exercise programs? Same problem. Ironically, I even had difficulty sticking with the techniques I learned in self-improvement courses. That's probably happened to you too. You read a book or attend a seminar and you're all fired up. "This stuff is terrific! I'm going right home to start this program immediately! I'm going to be disciplined and follow this system to the letter. This time it's going to be different."

Well, of course, it isn't different. The next night when you're supposed to begin taking the first step, your favorite TV program comes on. You know you should apply yourself, take some action, but—what, the heck—you worked hard today. You'll get started right after the show...or maybe tomorrow night.

And once again you've apparently changed your mind. I'm sure you've been as confused and frustrated by this pattern as I was. But you didn't really change your mind, any more than I did when each of my diets became history.

It just came to a critical point: it was time to empower the part of you that was going to decide what you do next, but you shifted gears and allowed the wrong part of you to "take the power" and make the decision. I know that sounds simple but, believe me, this is an insight that can really help, because it separates out a part of us so we can do battle with it.

In the next lesson, we're going to learn more about what this part of us is, and the battle we must engage in in order to conquer it.

Life Lesson 2

The Only Battle You Need To Win
Is The One Within

Where the Real Battles Are Fought

One time, back when I was speaking in four or five cities a week, I pulled my rented car up to a stop sign. While I was waiting for the traffic to clear, I happened to look over to my left. An old antique store caught my attention. It wasn't a very pretty place—rather old and run-down.

A huge sign leaned up against the store, an old gray board that someone had carved a saying in. If I live to be a hundred and fifty, I will never forget what that sign said. I guess I was just ready for it at the time, and those words burned into my soul. I went home and preached them so much to everybody I knew that, for my next birthday, my employees put them on a plaque and gave it to me. I still have it hanging on my office wall.

It said:

**Any man can conquer another man,
but the one who conquers himself is the true warrior.**

No truer words were ever spoken. That saying, passed on to me by some unknown benefactor, became my call to arms. It still serves as a constant reminder to me that the battleground of life is not "out there" with the world. Life's important battles are all fought within. If you are battling other people or outward circumstances, if you are fighting your battles in the external world, you can't possibly win because you don't even know where the battleground is. I really do mean the only person you need power over is you.

You Can't Fight Yourself

When we first realize that life's true battleground is within us and that in order to succeed in life we have to fight ourselves, we become very confused. And one of the main reasons we haven't had much success at winning these kinds of battles is that we, as human beings, simply do not have the ability to fight what we believe to be ourselves.

You see, if you think there is only one "you," then you're forced to *be* that "you" no matter what you're thinking at any given time. I know that sounds confusing, but let me show you what I mean. When I've just overeaten, I tend to be of the opinion that stuffing myself was the wrong thing to do, so at that point I resolve to stop all that foolishness and become slim and healthy. But by lunchtime tomorrow it seems that I've changed my mind and I no longer feel the same way. I have, instead, re-adopted the old set of priorities that caused me to overeat in the first place: How can I fight that? But more importantly, *why should I* fight that?

After all, I'm only doing what *I* want to do. And why shouldn't I use my own preferences as the criteria for living my life? Why shouldn't I do what I want to do now, rather than what I decided I wanted to do yesterday or last month? It's next to hopeless to engage in fighting a battle when there isn't really an enemy—instead it's just what I wanted yesterday trying to do battle with what I want now. And you know as well as I do that what I want now, always wins.

You see, your instinctive need for self-preservation will always keep you from diminishing or destroying that part of you that you're identifying with at the moment. No matter how hard you try, you can't conquer yourself—simply because you don't want to be conquered! As a healthy, normal person you will always be powerless to purposely diminish or destroy yourself in any way. And as long as you believe you *are* that portion of you that makes the wrong decisions and acts out of the wrong motivations, you will continue to do what it wants you to do.

Consider, for instance, the statement that you commonly make when you're feeling hunger: "I am hungry." Look at that

14

sentence again. It doesn't say you have hunger; it says you *are* hunger. And if "you are" hungry—that is, if you've made the hunger your identity—then you're powerless to fight it or in any way overcome it.

I think it's interesting that in the French language a similar statement would translate more like "I have hunger." Now that's a manageable problem!

We unwittingly place ourselves in a position of powerlessness when we use seemingly innocent phrases like "I am afraid" or "I am angry." If you *are* the anger, then your need for self-preservation will keep you from diminishing and certainly from conquering the source of your anger: you.

It is for this reason that we must separate ourselves into the different personalities that reside within each of us. A recovering alcoholic realizes that he's not the one that needs the drink, it's the disease of alcoholism that needs the drink. And as strange as this seemingly insignificant difference sounds, it makes the problem much more manageable.

By the same token, your fight to gain control over yourself will become much easier if you can find a way to separate the problem behavior from your identity, from who you really are. Then you can be free to do battle with that unwanted behavior...to diminish it and ultimately to overcome it.

Surprise! There Are Two of You
What's happening is that there's a battle going on between your two selves. Yes, that's right. There are two different versions of you. One of them always wants to implement your best intentions, and one of them seldom wants to implement them. There's a person inside me, for example, who always wants to eat correctly. But there's another one who always wants to pig out.

15

Our Higher and Lower Selves

Let me explain the two "me's" as I discovered them originally. You see, I found out that part of my personality is made up of my feelings—of my emotions, desires, and needs. This part of me is a short-term thinker. In fact, it's only interested in one time: right now. This emotional part of me is only interested in what feels the best for this moment and, frankly, it's not at all concerned with the consequences those actions might have. It only wants to find the pleasure button and push it constantly so I can have all the immediate gratification that's possible.

On the other hand, there's a part of me that's logical and rational. This side of me is a long-range thinker. It's the one that sets all of those worthwhile goals for the future because it realizes that if I will just do some things that my emotional side doesn't want to do for the moment, if I can keep myself from doing some things that my immediate desires would have me do, then I can have some things in the future that most people never find a way to have. It's the part of me that can figure out the *right* thing to do. It's my conscience, my better judgment, and my ability to know that even something that feels very good can be very wrong.

Once I realized that there were two personalities living in the one body called Joe Land, I started the process of learning how to separate the two.

I began by giving them names. For a long time I referred to my two sides as "Emotions versus Logic." As I became more familiar with the concept, I renamed them "Feelings versus Better Judgment." And while those were both correct to some degree, I later broadened the titles to my "Lower Self" and my "Higher Self".

These are totally opposite people, and yet both of them dwell within every one of us. It's as if you have two very different persons inside you. Freud referred to these aspects as our superego and our id, but there's no reason to get all fancy and complicated about it. I'll just refer to them from now on as our Higher Self and our Lower Self.

16

The Origins of Your Selves

When you were a young child—say one or two years old—you lived completely within your Lower Self. In fact, your Higher Self hadn't even awakened yet. As a toddler, you did not think in terms of fulfillment or serving others, or dedicating yourself to some purpose or higher calling. Your world revolved around "me, me, me." As a very young child, you really only have your Lower Self to base your actions on. And at that stage in your life, that's okay....it's normal.

But as you began to mature, another part of your personality began to emerge: your Higher Self. This is the expanding of your consciousness. It's at this point in your life that you realize that you can't live in a totally self-centered way. You become aware that responsibilities are as important as gratification.

With the continued growth of your Higher Self, your honor and integrity become more important to you, and, as this other person grows within you, it seems more and more that things that used to be perfectly acceptable are now inappropriate or even unacceptable.

But no matter how old you get, your Lower Self—that immature part of you that makes decisions based solely on feelings—never goes away. And we wouldn't want it to. While the Lower Self is less noble, you *need* that part of you. Without your emotions and feelings, your life would be boring indeed. No, you don't want to abandon your Lower Self. The idea, instead, is to strengthen your Higher Self so it can gain control and you can stop being a slave to the whims of the Lower Self.

Who Calls the Shots?

As you can see, your two selves are pulling you in opposite directions.

Your Higher Self wants to do what's in your best interest and in the best interest of others. It wants to do what's right. Your Lower Self just wants to do what feels good.

When you respond with anger, for instance, rather than reason, or allow yourself to think in terms of revenge or getting

17

back at someone rather than understanding them, you can be sure that the Lower Self has taken over and is running things. Anytime you make a decision based on what's good for you even though it's to the detriment of others, you're in your Lower Self. Your Lower Self tends to think in terms of your own selfish wants rather than the worthwhile considerations that are characteristic of your Higher Self.

Self-indulgence versus self-respect is the classic difference between the two, and with some objective observation of your thoughts and actions, you can begin to easily recognize which of your two selves is running your show at any given time.

I got a real-life demonstration of this the other day when I was watching one of those tabloid television talk shows. I have to tell you, I've always wondered why those people get on national television and say the things they say! I wouldn't be able to show my face in public. I can't imagine making those kinds of admissions and then going back to work...or even home for that matter. I'd have to enter one of those federal witness protection programs instead.

This particular show was about as bad as I've seen. The guests were a lady and her husband and her sister. It seems that this lady had caught her husband messing around with her sister.

Now, obviously this was not the smartest man in the world to begin with, but sleeping with his sister-in-law turned out not to be nearly as dumb as appearing before a nationally televised audience to talk about it. He found that out in a hurry as the studio audience chewed him up and spat him out. I felt sorry for him.

They also had a psychologist there, sitting in the front row. She was the expert who was supposed to shed some psychological light on these shenanigans and explain why and how it all happened. About midway through the show, someone in the audience asked our beaten-down playboy, "Well, why did you sleep with your wife's sister in the first place?" And as he opened his mouth to say something he thought would sound good—I don't think the guy had said anything honest all day long—this psychologist spoke up.

18

She said, "He did it because man is a sexual animal." And once that soaked in, she continued, "But, sir, man is also a civilized animal, and at some point your civility needs to grow to the point that it overcomes your sexuality." Now, are you ready for this? She then said: "Men devise a plan and then follow that plan. *Boys just do what feels good.*"

I really hated to hear that but, you know, she's exactly right. That *is* the difference between men and boys (and, in fairness, between women and girls). How many times have we been faced with the decision of whether to keep following the plan or deviate from it to do something that feels good? That's the classic struggle between the Higher Self and the Lower self.

Getting To Know The Other You

Now that you understand there are two of you instead of just one, the battle, that struggle to overcome a part of us, becomes much, much easier. It is almost impossible for you to overcome a part of you that you identify with, but now it's not "you" that's vacillating. Instead, it's a constant internal struggle between one side of you and another.

Back in my yo-yo dieting days, when I got hungry—when I *was* hungry and identified with the hunger—I was powerless to do anything about it. But if I realize that it's only my Lower Self that is a slave to hunger, I have the ability to refuse to *be* in my Lower Self and, instead, to step into and become that part of me that is convinced that my health is more important than satisfying the desire to eat. I can then take authority over that part of me that would cause me to do something the *real* me has decided not to do.

It may sound like I'm splitting hairs here, but believe me, I'm not. This is a tremendous source of power.

I make it a practice to run a few miles every morning to stay in shape. There are quite a few mornings I get up and say to myself, "I don't feel like running this morning." Now, if I make the mistake of thinking that was *me* speaking—if I thought I had changed my mind from the time I decided that a daily run was good for me—I would respond, "Okay, I won't run today." After all, I pretty well do what I want to do, and if I don't want to do it, I don't.

But now when I hear myself express a desire to slack off and not run today, I realize: That's not me, that's my Lower Self. There's no surprise here, it never wants to run—it doesn't like the way running feels. And as we know, the Lower Self is into feeling, so it comes as no great shock to me that that part of me voices regular opposition to the daily run.

So I just rededicate myself to the commitment by assuming the identity of my Higher Self, the person within me that has chosen the long-term benefits of that daily run. I then take authority over my Lower Self, treating it like a small child, and remind that part of me of why we've decided to run every day.

See how it works? It really does make "self-discipline" much easier. In fact, I'm not so sure that self-discipline, at least the way we have traditionally understood the term, even exists. And we certainly know that the people who still try to exert that old flawed concept of traditional self-discipline are probably going to fail—again.

Rather than continuing to try to exercise self-discipline in the traditional way—a concept we all agree doesn't work—let's move on to the next Life Lesson and learn more about how our mind works, so we can figure out how to keep it from working us!

Life Lesson 3

Your Behavior Won't Change...
Until You Do

Let's face it, we all do things we wish we didn't. I have a tendency to overeat. Twenty five percent of Americans still smoke cigarettes although we know that four hundred thousand people die each year from diseases related to smoking. Many of us drink too much. There are people who are hopeless nail biters and there are those among us that always show up late...the list is endless.

Or you might be among the countless people who occasionally fall victim to their emotions. A fit of anger can cause an otherwise completely rational person to make a spectacle of himself. Jealousy is probably as destructive a force as we know of, yet there are a lot of people who readily admit to being jealous but seem helpless to remove jealousy from their lives.

Yes, I'm afraid that all of us in our more honest moments have to admit that some portion of our life is out of control. We all do things we later wish we hadn't done. And every now and then we decide to eliminate some of the things we don't like about ourselves, but those efforts usually end in failure. Of course at that point we not only still have the undesirable behavior, we also have a renewed sense of helplessness because once again we tried to change...and couldn't.

Well, I have some good news and some bad news. First, the bad news. You're not *ever* going to be able to change your unwanted behaviors. If you could, you'd already have done it. In fact most of us have decided, after trying to make a change and failing at it enough times, to just give up and live with that part of us that we don't like.

But here's the good news. You don't have to change the *behavior*! All you have to do is find out *why* you do the things you do, and change that. And when you do, the offending behavior will change all by itself.

You see, trying to change your behavior is like sitting in a parked car and trying to make it go sixty miles an hour by grabbing the speedometer needle and moving it up to sixty. Does that accomplish anything? Of course not. On the other hand, if you understand enough about the car to start the engine, put it in gear, and push on the accelerator, you'll find that the speedometer will come up to sixty all by itself. And that's because a speedometer needle pointing to sixty is not a *cause*, it's an effect.

Our behavior is also an effect rather than a cause. That's why self-discipline alone usually ends up in failure, and our New Year's resolutions only last three days. It doesn't matter how hard you try to change if you're treating the symptoms instead of the disease itself. Attacking the problem in this way can't produce positive results, and destines us for failure. Behavior can be changed only by working on its root cause. And when you find that cause and change it, your behavior will change almost by itself.

There's a Thought Behind the Behavior

Back when I was on all those unsuccessful diets, I blew them all the same way. Let me set the scene for you. I'm three days into a new diet that I found in *Reader's Digest*, and things are going just fine, thank you very much. Of course, I am miserable, I am starving to death, and my life is barely worth living—but I have lost a quarter of a pound and so I'm right on track. Sound familiar?

And then, about eleven o'clock on the third morning, the worst thing that could conceivably happen to me happens: A life-size, Kodacolor image of a *cheeseburger* pops into my brain. I can see it right there in my mind's eye and I can almost smell the rich, hearty aroma.

Now, do you think I meant to think about food that day? Do you suppose I said, "Well, I believe I'll think about a

22

cheeseburger and torment myself awhile this morning?" Of course not. It just kind of slipped into my thoughts all by itself.

Now, you know as well as I do that if I had been able to remove that cheeseburger image from my mind and refuse to think about it, staying on my diet that morning would have been a piece of cake (well, you know what I mean).

But those thoughts that we leave unchecked and uncontrolled exert a powerful influence over us. And I suppose on some level I knew that, but back then I just didn't have the ability to control them. So instead of putting the cheeseburger out of my mind, which would have solved the problem, I *lusted* after the thing. I ate it over and over and over in my mind. I would dip the french fries in the ketchup and within an hour I would have worked myself into a feeding frenzy.

By now I bet you're thinking, "Oh, I know what happened next—he went on down and had a cheeseburger for lunch."

But please...you underestimate me. When I went to lunch that day, I ate one of those despicable little salads just like I promised myself I would.

I didn't go get the cheeseburger until about three that afternoon! By then those burger-thoughts had driven me crazy. And, of course, you're right—my diet was over.

That's the way it always works. You never do anything unless you first *think* about it. An action is *always* preceded by a thought. If you don't think about it, you don't do it.

So, now we know that our behavior is caused by our thoughts. And so it just makes sense that the way to change a behavior is to eliminate the thoughts that produce it.

But Who Decides What We Think About?

The problem is, we seldom consciously choose our next thought. You see, the conscious mind—that portion of the workings of your mind that you are aware of—is only capable of doing one thing at a time. Oh, it feels as though we can think about several things at once, but that's only because we have the ability to move very quickly from one thought to another, and that creates the illusion that we're thinking different things simultaneously. The truth of the matter is that most of the time we are incapable of consciously choosing what our next thought is going to be, because our conscious mind is busy—fully occupied with whatever we're thinking about right now.

So it's our subconscious that actually feeds us most of our thoughts. That's the reason it appears to us that thoughts "pop" into our minds from out of nowhere. But our subconscious doesn't just randomly choose the thoughts it gives to us. No, it carefully selects each thought it puts into our minds...based on our interests. Simply put, the subconscious feeds us thoughts that it believes we are interested in.

I'm sure that comes as no great shock to anyone. We all know, if we just reflect a bit, that we tend to think about the things we are interested in. If it's not interesting to us, we spend very little time thinking about it.

But how is it that your subconscious has come to know what you're interested in? It knows because, over the years, you have *programmed* it with your interests. You continually "teach" it what you like. Each time you make a conscious decision, your subconscious is put on notice that you are now more interested in this than you are in that. And because your subconscious works to serve you, it will continue to feed you thoughts about those things you've convinced it that you *want* to think about. These things we're interested in come in two flavors: positive and negative. Your positive interests include your goals, your dreams, and your desires, like that promotion you've been working so hard for, or the island in the Caribbean you sometimes dream about.

Probably the best example of how the subconscious can be programmed with a positive interest is someone who falls in love. A guy who falls in love in effect says, "Attention, subconscious mind! You see that attractive young lady over there? I don't want to think about anything but her until further notice." And the subconscious says, "You got it!" And then our friend begins to wander around in a blissful daze and is basically worthless for at least a month. You may as well give him sick leave until he decides that there are some other things in life that are also worth thinking about.

Then there are the negative interests, the things you've told your subconscious you want to spend plenty of time worrying about. They are the unwanted things you fear might come your way. You think about them because you are keenly interested in trying to keep them from happening—like getting fired from your job, getting audited because of a discrepancy on last year's tax return, or missing a meeting because you are caught in traffic.

If you think about it, you'll realize that your interests are nothing more than a reflection of your priorities. As we go through life we make countless decisions about what is and isn't important to us. Our interests are made up of those things we have decided are important. And, of course, as you place everything in your life in order of its importance to you, you've actually established your own unique set of *priorities*. The priorities that rank highest on your list are obviously the things that you're the most interested in. And that's how your subconscious knows which thoughts to feed you.

You see, each time you've made a decision and further developed your priorities—what's important or of interest to you—you've sent yet another signal to that powerful part of your mind that *is* capable of doing more than one thing at a time, and it then alters its idea of what you want to think about, and feeds you future thoughts accordingly.

It's All About What We Believe

But let's take a closer look at how the priorities that determine our interests are formed. They are determined by what we *believe*. As we go through life, we make literally thousands of decisions about which pieces of reality are important to us and which are not, based on our beliefs.

When I was a small boy, my first job was shining shoes in a barbershop not far from where I lived. My mother pointed out to me, after I'd worked there for a while, that when I first saw someone I always looked at his shoes. She was right. You could depend on me to display that behavior consistently because it resulted from what I was interested in.

You see, I was always, even in my childhood, a bit of an entrepreneur. Even back then making money was important to me. Most of the time it was more important than playing with my friends or playing games. Now, during my shoe-shining career I had obviously come to the conclusion (belief) that shining shoes was the best way I could make the money that was so important to me. That's why I displayed an interest in everyone's shoes—because if someone needed a shine, I could turn that need into some money!

Now as simple as all this sounds, it gives us a perfect illustration that behavior is nothing more than a result of what you believe. I don't think I ever sat down and *decided* to look at everyone's shoes. It was a natural behavior that accompanied my interest in the money I could make if the next person I saw needed a shine.

The saying is true that to a hammer everything in the world looks like a nail. And you view the world in a way that fits your beliefs about what it's all about...and what you're all about.

From Beliefs to Behavior

Okay, let's take a look then at the completed chain of events.

Beliefs →Priorities →Interests →Thoughts →Behavior

Our behavior is created by our thoughts and our thoughts are a result of our interests. When we couple that with the fact that our interests are nothing more than a reflection of our priorities and that those priorities result from what we believe, I think you can see the real reason I was seventy five pounds overweight.

Back then I hadn't discovered a better reason for living than self-gratification. I was in constant pursuit of pleasure. That was my *belief* about what life was all about. Now, add that to the fact that I grew up in an old-fashioned country home where life was

26

built around meals, and it doesn't take a rocket scientist to figure out that eating soon became my favorite recreation. And because I didn't know any better, recreation—enjoying myself—was what I lived for.

As a family we didn't talk much about health or the benefits of proper eating. We were strictly a "pass the biscuits" bunch of folks. And we were not the kind of people who placed little morsels of food in our mouths and engaged in a lot of stimulating conversation while waving an empty fork around to emphasize a point. If we said something during a meal it was more along the lines of, "Man, that fried chicken is good tonight." (Of course you could barely understand that statement because the mouth that said it was crammed full of the subject of it.)

What I'm trying to say is that by the time I was grown, food—good old *fattening* food—was about as important as anything in my life. I was a confirmed recreational eater, and when you took away my ability to stuff myself three times a day with that good ole greasy home cooking, you took away my happiness. And, of course, because the taste of fattening food was more important to me than my health, my energy level, my appearance, or even my self-esteem, I thought about it...a lot.

That's why the thought of that cheeseburger always haunted me later on as I tried to change that part of my behavior. All I was doing was thinking about what *I* was interested in. And, of course, what I was interested in was my number one priority— food!

Now I'm sorry, but you will never be able to rid yourself of an unwanted behavior *unless you change the belief that creates that behavior.* I was never able to change my eating habits until I changed my basic beliefs about what was important to me and what wasn't. When you harbor the belief that satisfying your desire for large amounts of fattening food is more important than all the things you lose when you give in to that desire, you may as well not even try to change your behavior, because what you do is always a reflection of what you believe. Your behavior is nothing more than *the manifestation of your beliefs. If you want*

27

to change your behavior, you must change what you believe. And then, like the speedometer needle, your behavior will adjust itself accordingly—automatically.

Life Lesson 4

Most Habits Have Outlived Their Usefulness

When I first realized that all of my actions resulted from my beliefs, I was certain I was on my way to gaining control of my behavior. I was smoking about a pack of cigarettes a day back in those days, and I reasoned that I hadn't been able to quit smoking because, deep down, my need to fulfill the desire for those cigarettes was overriding the fact that they were causing me harm. In other words, my belief system was structured in a way that made the cigarettes more important to me than my health.

So I simply made a new decision. One day I sat down and rearranged my priorities. Yes, I thought, my lower self does enjoy smoking. But I remembered how I felt after running into a man I hadn't seen in several years, in the lobby of a doctor's office, and learning that he was suffering from acute emphysema. He had looked at me and said, in a voice that was barely audible between labored, shallow breaths, "If you're smart, you'll never smoke another cigarette." Well, I decided to put stopping that from happening to me on a more important level than satisfying my desire for cigarettes.

Okay, now I've done it! I have changed my beliefs. Now my health is more important to me than smoking. I will quit immediately!

Well, you can imagine how dismayed I was the next afternoon when I gave in and lit up a cigarette! Then I figured out that even though I was on the right track, there was one more very important factor that I hadn't yet considered. You see, my smoking had become a *habit.*

That's when I learned that just making a new decision and altering my belief system wouldn't get the job done alone. Because, you see, our behavior doesn't necessarily stem from our *current* beliefs. No, I'm afraid our behavior is for the most part a result of our past beliefs, because it was from those beliefs that we formed the habits that control so much of what we do today.

How Our Habits Are Developed

I mentioned in the last Life Lesson that our conscious mind is capable of thinking only one thought, or attending to only one matter, at a time. Yet we all know that real life often demands that we do several things simultaneously.

Fortunately, all our actions don't require our conscious attention, because if they did, chewing gum and walking at the same time would literally be impossible! That's why we call upon the subconscious, the part of our mind that we are not aware of, to handle some of our actions for us. This allows our conscious mind to focus on more demanding concerns.

Habits are the daily routines or behaviors the subconscious carries out in order to free the conscious mind for activities that require conscious thinking and decision making. These are the things we teach our subconscious mind to do for us— automatically. We walk by habit. If you don't believe that, remember the last time you stepped off a curb without realizing it was there? Only then did your walking "get your attention." Up until that point, the movement of your legs had been totally automatic and you were thinking about something else altogether.

In fact, virtually everything physical we do is done subconsciously. Do you remember the first time you tried to drive a car? Most of us do, especially if the car was one of those dreaded standard shifts rather than an automatic. The car I learned in was, and I remember trying desperately to carry out all the things I was expected to do. Learning the gear positions. Shifting with my hand while working the clutch with my foot. Switching back and forth between the brake and accelerator pedals—all the while steering and keeping my eye on the road in front of me and remembering to glance at the rearview mirror!

I don't know about you, but after my first lesson I decided there was no way I could do so many things at once. I was convinced a piece of my brain was missing—the piece that lets you learn how to drive. But as soon as my subconscious began to take over some of those duties, and do them all at once, driving became much easier. Now most of my driving has been taken over by my subconscious—it's become a habit. That allows my conscious mind to focus on the important matters that need my conscious attention, like pedestrians and other vehicles.

And, of course, you drive by habit, too. Do you consciously remember to use the turning signal each time you turn a corner? Rarely, I'll bet. Don't you lock and unlock the doors without thinking about it? If you've been driving for very long, you have no problem lowering the volume on the car radio while negotiating a curve and carrying on a conversation with someone in the seat next to you. The ability of your subconscious to carry out all those physical actions allows your conscious mind to carry on the conversation.

We rely heavily on habits because we're simply not capable of making a conscious choice about when and how we do each of the thousands of things we need to do each day. Instead, we make those decisions one by one over a period of years. Then, as we adopt each of these patterns as habits, our subconscious takes over. Once that happens, most of us don't ever even consider acting any differently. By the time we reach adulthood, most of the habits we've taught our subconscious have become so deeply ingrained that they stay with us for life.

Most of Our Thinking Is Habit, Too

Most of us tend to think of habits as being only behavioral, but our thoughts follow habitual patterns as well. Most of the thoughts you think today, you also thought yesterday—and the day before, and the day before that.

Let's face it, most of us do the same things every day. The things we do, the decisions we make, what we say to other people, all come about in the same way as we live our lives, day after day.

We've all developed what we believe to be the most efficient ways of thinking and carrying on our own inner mental dialogue as we handle our daily situations, and we have long since made these inner activities habitual patterns of thinking.

If you're a chess player, you've come to favor certain strategies that seem to work best for you. You've actually developed a certain way of thinking for most of the situations you find yourself in as you play the game. They have become your habitual patterns of thought—your style of playing chess.

When mental and physical habits work together, here's what happens. Imagine a smoker who is over at a friend's house having a heated political argument. His friend's a Republican, he's a Democrat, and they're telling each other what's best for the country. Our smoker is in the middle of making a point, maybe even in midsentence, when suddenly a tiny bit of anxiety pops into the back of his mind. His conscious mind—which, at the moment is busy presenting his side of the argument—is unaware of that little feeling. But the subconscious recognizes it, immediately jumps into action, and begins reviewing possible responses. It considers options all the way down the line, until it decides that the correct response is to smoke a cigarette. Now, at this point this guy doesn't know that he's about to light up! His subconscious has made the decision to smoke a cigarette, but *he* hasn't been informed. That's why at the end of the evening, he looks at the ashtray full of cigarette butts and the empty package crumpled nearby and says: "I can't believe how many cigarettes I've smoked! I've got to quit smoking!"

This happened because some time back, our friend taught his subconscious when he wanted to smoke. He had his first cigarette by making a conscious decision to light up. He had the second cigarette by conscious decision as well, and many more. But when his subconscious observed time after time that he always responded to anxiety-provoking situations in the same way—by having a cigarette—his subconscious said: "I think I've got it! You want to respond to that feeling with a cigarette? No problem. Leave it to me. You won't even have to think about it anymore." And the subconscious then took over the decision making process, turning the response into a habit.

Even Our Emotions Are on Automatic Pilot

In fact, even our emotional responses to the daily occurrences in our lives become habitual. For example, there probably are certain situations that automatically make you angry. Maybe you feel irritated whenever you stand in a line. There you are at the bank or post office, and when you step to the rear of the line, you instantly feel annoyed and resentful. And you'd probably feel the same way even if you weren't particularly rushed or tired. So where does the feeling come from? It has become habitual for you. At times in the past, you chose to react with anger and resentment at having to stand in line and wait for other people. And when you responded that way often enough to teach that attitude to your subconscious, it took over and now does the job of bringing forth that anger all by itself.

Other things that happen may instantly embarrass you or make you happy or whatever. But when you think about it, how many of those feelings were really appropriate responses to the actual situations that caused them? You might actually be associating a particular aroma or song with a happy, or sad, time in your childhood. And this is true even if we can't remember *why* they are causing us to feel that way. They've simply triggered the habitual emotional responses we've learned in the past, ones that have now become automatic.

That's the main reason we get upset many times at minor things which, after some thought, we realize didn't deserve anywhere near such an extreme response. Let's face it. Once you teach yourself that anger is the appropriate response to a given situation, you don't need a valid reason to get upset. For the most part, our emotional responses are on automatic pilot.

33

It's Time To Question Our Habits

There's an old story I love. It seems that one day a man was sitting in his kitchen, watching his wife getting a ham ready to go into the oven. After fifteen years of marriage, he had watched this same ritual hundreds of times. She cut both ends off the ham, placed the ham in the pan, put the two ends on top of it, and slid the whole thing into the oven.

"Why do you do that?" he asked.

"Why do I do what?" she replied.

"Why do you always cut the ends off your hams before you put them in the oven? You've done that for years."

She said: "Well, come to think of it, I don't know. My mother taught me how to cook, and she always did it that way. I'm sure there's a good reason, but I can't remember what it is."

"Call your mother and find out," the husband said. "I'm curious."

So his wife got her mother on the phone. "Mom, why do we cut the ends off our hams before we put them in the oven?"

Her mother replied, "Well, I don't know why you do it, dear, but my pan was too small for a whole ham to fit in."

We do things because we've been trained to do them, whether there's a reason for it or not. Oh, there may have been a reason initially. But the biggest problem with habits is that all too often they continue on long after they've outlived their usefulness. There are literally hundreds of things we do, say, and think every day that no longer have any real purpose in our lives. We're now encumbered by these pointless habits, not realizing that they take up a great deal of our time and energy. And they often interfere with *our* current values and priorities.

When we were young, we borrowed many of our habits and beliefs from other people, especially our parents. And even those who were fortunate enough to have two kind, loving, wonderful parents were inadvertently misprogrammed in some areas of their lives. When we were small, these towering people were all-wise and all-knowing. Their beliefs became our beliefs—full strength—because we weren't yet able to formulate our own. For the early part of our lives, everything they told us went, unfiltered and unjudged, straight into our subconscious minds. It wasn't until we had already undergone years of programming that we realized that our parents weren't perfect. And let's face it, as great as they may have been, some of the things they taught us...came straight from their Lower Self.

And even those habits which we taught to ourselves may have been formed as a result of beliefs that came from our Lower Self's emotional priorities rather than from the beliefs that represent our current values. But you have the option of making new decisions—decisions from your Higher Self—and establishing new beliefs. However, deciding to act differently now doesn't help you unless you take the time to install the new belief where it can do you the most good: in the source of your actions—your habits. And you can do that. All it takes is for you to consciously reinforce and stress the new priority long enough for a new habit to form. Otherwise, you continue to play life out from the habits created by old decisions, your old programming. When you say, "I wish I didn't act like this, but I guess that's just the way I am," you're *wrong*. That's not the way you are—that's just the way you've programmed yourself.

But the good new is, you can *reprogram* yourself in a brand new way... and I'll show you how in the next lesson.

Life Lesson 5

If It Was Easy,
Everybody Would Be Doing It

I used to work with a real estate developer in Albuquerque, New Mexico, named Griff Pickard. His favorite saying was, "Well, if it was easy, everybody would be doing it." That was always his response to anyone who came to him complaining about how difficult one of his objectives was to meet. And you know, in a strange way those words had an encouraging effect on all of us. Somehow they gave us a reason to overcome our difficulties. His little saying always put our situation into perspective and reminded us that we could be winners if we realized that we just needed to hang in there a little longer and try a little harder than everybody else did.

Well, let me say those words to you. I realize that what I'm about to tell you to do will seem foreign in many ways. I know it will take some energy and you'll have to put forth a good deal of effort. But, my friend, if it was easy, everybody would be doing it. Everybody would be in total control. Everybody would be slim, fit, courageous, patient, honorable, determined, dependable, principled, mature, and successful in every area of their lives. And, of course, we know they're not. But *you* can be all these things...if you really want to.

Prove You Really Want It

You see, there's no question that you can bring about real change in your life. But while everyone *wants* to change at least something about who and what they are, very few people find a way to get it done. Their attempts end in failure for two reasons. First of all, they don't know how. Most people just don't know enough about how their mind works to gain enough control of it to make significant changes. Well, I can solve that problem for

37

you. In the pages that follow I'm going to give you the methods and techniques that can put you in total control.

But the second one is tougher to overcome. It is simply that they don't have enough *desire*. Make no mistake, it won't help you to know *how* changes are made if you don't sincerely *want* to make them. Desire will serve as the fuel that powers your quest for change. Your success in putting the insights I will give you into action will depend on, more than anything else, your determination and persistence. So the first thing you must do is make a quality commitment...to yourself. Decide once and for all that *you are worth the effort* it will take to have the kind of life you want. You see, staying committed and remaining convinced that you are worthy to have what you've set out to get is most of the battle. After you get over that hill, it's simply a matter of execution.

Making Your Goal #1

You can attain your desires if you recognize that what's involved is a *reprogramming* process. The challenge before you is to consciously enforce the attitude and behavior that reflect your new belief for long enough to override the programming controlling your old habit that's there now.

You have to convince your subconscious that you're serious about wanting a change, or it will oppose you. You see, your subconscious is your servant, and it faithfully does for you the things you've asked it to—but it needs to be sure you're really asking. Because initially, your subconscious treats your new decisions and the new beliefs that result from them just like you treat your children when they ask for something they've never asked for before.

Let's say you have a four-year-old who announces at the dinner table: "I want a new tricycle, a red one just like Bobby's." What is your first response? You say, "Uh-huh," and forget all about it. Why? Because he's already asked for about fifteen other things today, and he's already forgotten about every one of them. You learned a long time ago that if you run out and buy everything he says he wants, most of the stuff will end up in the closet that's full of the junk he already has. But does that mean you ignore everything he says, and never get him anything he wants? Of course not. So how does your four-year-old go about getting that tricycle?

Persistence. By proving that he *really* wants it. He asks tomorrow for that red tricycle, and the next day, and then again that afternoon...and one of these days, you know as well as I do that kid is going to have himself a red tricycle. All he has to do is exert some patience and a *lot* of tenacity.

That's exactly what you need to show to your subconscious when you make a new decision. Let's say you decide (again) to start an exercise program. Starting tomorrow, you're going to jog several miles every morning before breakfast.

How does your subconscious respond? "Yeah, sure. I've heard that one before." But you *can* convince your subconscious that you are serious. You only need to prove to it that this is not just another one of your whims—that your priorities really have changed.

I remember when I decided to start using the seat belt in my car. I had been sitting on the thing for years, but I suppose all those road signs and television advertisements finally got to me and so I made another one of those *decisions.* I decided that the seat belt was now important to me and that I needed to buckle it each and every time I got into the car. And I started doing just that.

Of course, there were times in the beginning when I forgot to fasten my seat belt and I would later find myself driving down the street without it buckled, but as time went on, I got better and better at reminding myself to take care of this little chore before starting the engine. Then, before long, there were times that I would get in the car while deep in thought or when I was involved in a conversation with someone, and when I finally consciously remembered the seat belt, I reached for it only to find that it was already buckled! My subconscious was beginning to catch on.

I noticed another interesting thing: It wasn't long after I decided to start buckling up that I began to hear the "Fasten Seat Belt" buzzer. I had totally forgotten that my car even had one. I had trained myself not to hear it. But, when I again became aware of it, every time I got in the car the buzzing just about drove me nuts, and I immediately had to buckle my seat belt to stop it! Now that's a pretty dramatic demonstration of how much our habits govern our perceptions.

You see, part of the training I put my subconscious mind through when I learned to drive early on was that buckling my seat belt wasn't important. Once my subconscious got the idea that I didn't want to buckle the seat belt and had no use for the buzzer, it tuned it out, and I stopped hearing it. But, during the transition time when I was reprogramming my habit, for the first time in years I was aware of the sound. My subconscious allowed me to hear the buzzer because now I *wanted* to be reminded. That's how deeply our habits are ingrained in us and how much they control our daily lives: We've even taught ourselves what to be aware of and what to ignore. And you usually can't change a habit until you regain an awareness of what you're now ignoring.

I'm sure you've tried to replace undesirable habits with better ones in the past, and when you did you encountered a lot of internal resistance. After seeing how hard the change was, you may have rationalized: "Well, this change is just contrary to my nature," or "It feels so unnatural to do this, I suppose I'm just not the kind of person who can."

Granted, change seems very difficult. But the resistance you feel isn't you, *it's your past programming.* It's your *habits*—what you've taught yourself to do and think and feel. But doesn't it make sense that if you were able to program yourself in the past, you can *reprogram* yourself now?

Let me show you how.

40

Phase One: Make a New Decision

If you want to alter your habits, the first thing you have to do is make a new decision. Making this kind of decision, though, is more difficult than it sounds.

Making a new decision involves stretching your thinking into a new set of rules and a new way of looking at things. It means uprooting all the limitations, assumptions, and perceptions that are part of the problem you're trying to eliminate. To make a new decision and enforce it, you're going to have to change one or more of your priorities. You need to decide that your Higher Self's version of the issue at hand is the one that's going to prevail...the one you're going to identify with.

The mechanism you use to make that decision feels like you're simply sitting down and weighing the benefits on both sides of a particular issue, and making a new decision about what is most important to you. Let me give you an example.

If you're someone who has a problem with food—if you're overweight—there's only one thing you have to do in order to completely solve your problem. You must rearrange your priorities so that *you are more important than the food!* Let me show you how this worked in my life.

For years I was a recreational eater—it was the biggest pleasure in my life. While shaving in the morning, I would think about what I was going to have for lunch. I was an absolute slave to food. Food was my best friend. I ate for recreation. I ate when I was depressed. I even ate when I was depressed about being overweight!

One day I realized the truth: Food was not my best friend, it was my enemy. It was robbing me of my health, my energy, and my self-esteem. It was easy for anyone to see that the harm my eating habits were causing me far outweighed the passing pleasures I received from them. I decided it was time to stop.

That was the point in my life when I became totally fed up with being fat. That happened when I made the decision to change my priorities.

After carefully and objectively weighing the benefits and drawbacks of both sides of the issue, I simply decided that my

41

health, energy level, appearance, well-being, and self-control were more important to me than the taste of fattening food. I was now armed with a new belief, one which became the basis of an important new priority for me. You see, I *decided* to become fed up with my eating habits. I *decided* my present situation was no longer tolerable. I *decided* I was sick of being fat.

I purposely changed my beliefs about both what was acceptable to me and how capable I was of doing something about it. From those decisions came a strength and resolve I had never known before.

Phase Two: Create a New Image

The next thing you need to do is come up with a new visual image, one that represents your new priority.

It's really important that you find a way to keep from dwelling on and savoring all those wishful thoughts of whatever it is your Lower Self is having to give up. Did you ever hear the story about the little boy who was told *not* to think about a pink elephant? Well, it seems the harder he tried not to think of a pink elephant, the more he found it was all he could think about. And I've heard otherwise rational people say, based on that principle, that it is impossible to keep from thinking about something because the very fact that you're concerned with *not* thinking of it constantly brings it to mind.

I've found that nothing could be further from the truth. If the little boy in the story wanted to avoid thinking about a pink elephant, he could easily have done so by simply thinking about a *blue* one! So, you see, you need a vivid replacement image to insert into your mind anytime you find yourself having thoughts that reflect your old priorities.

Do you remember a couple of lessons ago, when I told you about the mental picture of a cheeseburger that always led to the destruction of my diet programs? Well, let me tell you how I finally won that battle. After I made the decision that my body was more important to me than the taste of all those old favorite foods, I dreamed up a visual image to represent my new preference. I vividly imagined myself slim and trim, with a body to kill for. I saw myself holding my head up high, reflecting the fact that I was completely in control, a true warrior who had brought his enemy—those terrible eating habits—into complete submission. I was now armed with a new priority and a vision to represent it.

Phase Three: Engage in Conscious Manual Override

Now you're ready to replace the old, undesirable habit with one that's in keeping with your new decision. The idea is to reprogram your subconscious to automatically feel, think, and act in harmony with the behavior patterns you've decided to put into place. I call this "conscious manual override" because during this critical period you're going to take *conscious* charge of the part of your behavior you're working on. In my case, it was my choice of foods and how much of them I ate. Over the course of my life, I had formed my habits by teaching my subconscious that big, fattening meals were more important to me than the benefits of eating correctly. So at that point, my old set of priorities was firmly in control of my eating habits. Recreational eating was a high priority for me, and my habits dutifully carried out that priority.

So, I temporarily relieved my subconscious of the responsibility of running that part of my life. I began to *consciously* make myself think the kinds of thoughts that promoted the new plan, and I started demonstrating the new behavior so that my subconscious could learn that a new set of priorities was in place and that those priorities called for a radically different way of living...both internally and externally.

Conscious manual override is simply when you take over some activity of your life and purposely do it a different way—a way that matches a new priority you've just put in place—and insist upon thinking and acting that way until you've replaced the old habit with the new one.

43

Now, I must tell you that the first forty or fifty times I replaced the picture of that cheeseburger with an image of the new, improved version of me, the cheeseburger instantly came back and clobbered it. You see, when I first started projecting the new picture, my subconscious must have said: "What's going on here? Put that cheeseburger back up there. He loves them!"

But remember the little boy who wants the tricycle? Well, through that same kind of repetition and persistence I did, indeed, replace my terrible eating habits. I kept replacing the picture of that cheeseburger with a picture of the new, slimmer me, and, at some point in the process, something in the back of my mind said, "Wait a minute, I think the old boy's really changed his mind on this one."

Interesting phrase, "change your mind"—and, you know, that's exactly what we want to do. And I've learned that one of the best ways to do it is to begin a dialogue between your Higher Self and your Lower Self.

Assume a Different Identity

Paul Harvey, the radio commentator, tells a story about a man who was in a shopping mall when he heard a woman behind him say, "No! You're not having any more candy and that's final!" The man didn't notice anything unusual about that until he turned around and saw that the woman who had made the statement was all alone! That's right, she was laying down the law to her Lower Self because she was smart enough to realize that if she wasn't strong enough to deny herself the candy, nobody else was going to. And, besides, you can bet her Lower Self didn't feel strange about speaking up. I'll promise you there was a little voice inside her yelling, "Let's have some more candy!"

You already have conversations with yourself. The problem is, they're usually one-sided. *Why not give your Higher Self a voice?* You'll automatically strengthen it by allowing it to have its say, for it's impossible for you to speak in behalf of your

44

Higher Self without actually stepping *into* your Higher Self and assuming that identity. And since your subconscious is always watching, and it mimics everything you do, it's wise to give it lots of instruction and practice in being your Higher Self.

In fact, the three most powerful words the Higher Self can say to the Lower Self are "I would rather" These words, ordinary as they may sound, are your means of shifting into your Higher Self. Saying them serves as a formal announcement that your better judgment is taking over.

The more time you spend in your Higher Self, the more you identify with—and become—your Higher Self. And what happens to the Lower Self? The same thing that happens to anything that's neglected: It begins to wither. It loses its strength. The more time you spend in your Higher Self, the weaker the Lower Self becomes.

When my Lower Self would start to nag me with a cheeseburger deluxe image, I'd replace that image with the representation of my new priority—the slim, healthy, attractive me—and say, "*I would rather* be like this than eat that cheeseburger." That picture of myself became a reflection of my new dream, my new priority, my new goal. I stayed conscious of the reality that this was actually an ongoing battle between fattening food and the body I wanted. And I found I could stay on the winning side by enthusiastically visualizing my new goal and saying to myself, "*I would rather* have a healthier me."

It Won't Happen Overnight

But don't expect to successfully install a new habit if you try the "I would rather" technique only once or twice. You must continue the process until the "I would rather" priority becomes an automatic response instead of one you have to constantly monitor and enforce on a conscious level.

There's a popular story among speakers about a guy who conducted an experiment to find out how long it would take to form a new habit. I have no idea whether the story is true or not,

45

but it's interesting and it does lend some insight into how the process works.

It seems that this fellow moved the trash can in his office from the left side of his desk to the right side. The first few days he found himself throwing his trash on the floor, from habit, right where the old trash can used to be. He would then have to pick it up, engage in conscious manual override, and consciously throw the trash into the can in its new location. He said he had to pick up crumpled paper off the floor for twenty days. But on the twenty first day, he noticed that his subconscious had learned the new location and he was throwing his trash in the repositioned receptacle without having to think about it.

Does that mean that all of your habits can be changed in twenty one days? No. You see, there's no emotional attachment to which side of the desk your trash can sits on. There is, however, a lot of emotion involved in the habits we've formed over the years from the desires of our Lower Self. These deeply entrenched habits take longer to change, because the resistance level is greater. But rest assured that the resistance does diminish as time goes by, growing less significant every day you keep the plan in force.

Change Your Habits One at a Time

The fact that this process has to be carried out at the conscious level means you can't change many habits at once. Indeed, it's much better to tackle them one at a time.

Start with the easiest one to change so you'll have a victory behind you that will build confidence in your ability to change. Once you learn to expect the resistance and realize that it will continue to lessen if you stay in charge, the task becomes much more manageable. Even though it feels unnatural, difficult, and slow, it does get easier. As you convince your subconscious that your priorities have really changed, it will begin to serve you willingly according to your new instructions.

Remember, consistency and persistence are the keys to making this method work for you. If implementing the new plan is only important to you part of the time, your old habits will defeat you. The need for change must become a major priority in your life. Your desires can only give you the power to change if you keep them at the *forefront* of your thinking. The words "I would rather" need to become a constant part of your inner dialogue...even after you're tired of hearing yourself say them. And if you stay with the reprioritizing process in every kind of circumstance, you'll soon find that you really can have, do, or be virtually anything you want.

PART TWO

The Power
of Your Beliefs

Life Lesson 6

Sometimes "Hitting Bottom" is Just What You Need

We've all experienced that unique time or two in our lives when making big decisions and bringing about dramatic changes was easy and natural for us. Many of us have had, for instance, at some point in our lives, a profound spiritual experience. When that happened, major changes in our beliefs came about without much effort on our part at all.

Or you may have known a confirmed bachelor who was totally committed to staying single for the rest of his life until he met a woman who was so special to him that his views on the subject of marriage changed radically, and, of course, his behavior followed suit.

But what if there's a change we'd *like* to make...when we don't have the emotional benefit of an earth-shaking experience ? Obviously we need to find a way to push our own buttons—to take control of our lives so that rather than having to wait for something profound to happen to push us into the change, we can *decide* to bring it about on our own.

But these kinds of life-changing decisions call for radically new ways of thinking, and it takes a lot of energy and effort to carry them out. Because we know it's such a big job, we don't ever seem to get to the place in our lives when *now* is the time to go to that much trouble. Most people have to reach a point of being in so much pain that our of sheer frustration and desperation they finally decide a change *has* to be made. And that's what allows an alcoholic, say, rather than a compulsive overeater, to embark on the road to recovery.

You see, there's a big difference between an alcoholic and a compulsive overeater that boils down to more than just the nature of the addiction. Of the two, the alcoholic is more likely to reach a point where the pain of his or her addiction exceeds the pleasure. After all, people who are addicted to alcohol can lose jobs, destroy marriages, even end up in jail. Thus those who are able to overcome this addiction usually do so because, at some point, they are forced to admit that they are literally destroying their lives. It's under this kind of duress that the alcoholic is able to make a life-changing decision, rearrange his or her priorities, and stop drinking.

But most of us find it impossible to make the life-changing decisions we'd like to make, because we're simply not experiencing enough emotional and physical pain to force that kind of decision on ourselves. Unlike alcoholics, people who are addicted to fattening foods don't suffer all that much, especially if they only gain a few extra pounds each year. The ill effects of their addiction are barely noticeable. Usually they don't have any day-to-day awareness that they've become more susceptible to heart attack, stroke, and other diseases. And although their energy level has declined considerably and they don't feel as good as they used to, the deterioration of their health and energy has been so gradual that they haven't really noticed the change. Ironically, it's these kinds of people, rather than, say, alcoholics, who will often have a harder time gaining control of their addiction, because the addiction isn't providing them with enough adversity to force them to change.

We Could All Stand a Little Adversity

In fact, you might say that in many ways we Americans are suffering from a severe *lack* of adversity. It usually takes adversity to create a compelling need, and unless you feel the need to change you will rarely expend the energy even to give it a try. So, most of us maintain the status quo, which, if not particularly fulfilling or meaningful, is at least comfortable and familiar. A moderate level of discontent simply doesn't provide us with enough incentive to go to the trouble to bring about a change. A person who has hit bottom, however, is in a totally different situation. This person has an overwhelming need to find a way to make things better.

I'm sure you can remember a time you hit bottom. I'll bet that experience had a dramatic effect on your priorities, on your thinking, on the types of decisions you were willing to make in your life. No doubt there's some part of your life now that's radically different than it used to be, all because at some time you hit bottom and decided you *had* to make a change in that area of your life. This is the kind of truly life-changing decision we need to find a way to bring about any time we see the need for it.

Where the Bottom Is... Depends on You

Of course, different people find the bottom at different levels. How far you have to sink before you reach the bottom depends on two things. The first is how much adversity you are willing to endure. In other words, how high is your pain threshold? Sadly, most people are willing to accept tremendous amounts of adversity before they're willing to shift the way they think. For the "hitting bottom" springboard process to work for you, you must come to believe that the discomfort of your present situation is worse than what you'll have to go through to achieve a "cure."

A nineteen-year-old out on his own for the first time who has to sleep in his car for a week because he didn't go find a job, finds making a life-changing kind of decision much easier than the rest of the employed world. Suddenly, he's painfully aware of the reality that there's no longer anybody willing to pay his rent for him—he's really on his own! In that first cold and uncomfortable night, he gains a lot of maturity, and it happens for one simple reason: The situation is just not acceptable to him. Our teenager starts to say things like, "There *must* be a better way!" Followed by, "I will never put myself in this position again." And, sure enough, he manages to find a job, appreciate it, and work hard enough to keep it. What a change from last week, when he couldn't even get himself out of bed to go look for work. So there's really something to be said for the effectiveness of hitting bottom.

I've attended quite a few Alcoholics Anonymous meetings, not because I'm an alcoholic, but because I'm very interested in how those folks fight their battle. You see, they're among the very few of us who are aware that life's real battles are inward, and that there's a part of them that they must fight and conquer.

Every recovering alcoholic I've ever known has, at some time in the past, come to a place he calls "hitting the wall." I kept hearing people stand up in AA meetings and say things like: "I was an absolute slave to alcohol. I was drunk and unable to do anything about it for twenty six years. I tried thousands of times to stop drinking and I couldn't. And then, on September 19, 1986, I hit the wall...and I haven't had a drink since."

"Wow!" I thought, "that's pretty heavy stuff. This 'hitting the wall' business must really be something! But what is it? How does it work? How does it make such a radical difference in their lives?"

Well, I think I've figured it out. You see, hitting the wall—the "hitting bottom" experience for an alcoholic—is when the alcoholic really decides, deep inside him, that the drink he wants so badly is no longer worth the price he has to pay for it. And in that instant, he changes a number of the parameters his life is based on. He has just uprooted an entire set of core priorities and replaced them with new ones. Yes—that's the instant the alcoholic becomes a recovering alcoholic. At that point, he becomes a person who has the strength to fight off his desire for alcohol. The need for the drink isn't as strong now, because it's no longer his top priority. Under his new belief structure, maintaining his dignity, holding his family together, and gaining peace of mind have suddenly replaced alcohol at the top of his list of priorities.

The second factor that determines where the bottom is for you depends on your level of self-confidence. You can benefit from reaching the bottom *only if you believe that it's within your power to change your circumstances and "crawl back out."* People who hit bottom without at least some minimal faith in their ability to change things will, instead of being empowered by the experience, see themselves as helpless victims and sink even deeper into despair.

And, of course, whether or not you believe yourself capable of improving your situation is a product of your personal beliefs. You may, indeed, be *able* to do even more than you believe you can. But without a belief in that ability it won't do you any good...because you'll never have the courage to try.

I think most of us realize that, as a rule, we *can* do what we *think* we can do. The old saying that "If you think you can, or if you think you can't, you're right" is true.

The Path of Least Resistance

There's another way to look at how to hit bottom and decide to make the change to a more desirable behavior. You see, by the time we reach one of these bottoms in our lives, there are no good choices left. For instance, to the person who's become desperate to remove procrastination from his or her life, the choices are clear...but not much fun. He or she realizes, "I either have to go through the pain of making myself into an active person, whether I feel like it or not, or I must continue to suffer the hardships that my procrastination causes me." Clearly this is a choice between two evils.

We tend to make those kinds of choices by following what is called the path of least resistance. In his book, *The Path of Least Resistance*, Robert Fritz claims that everything in the world follows the easiest course. The wind blowing between buildings follows the path of least resistance; so does electricity moving through a computer or a light bulb, and water flowing along a riverbed. Fritz goes on to point out another unchangeable fact: Human behavior also follows the path of least resistance. We are who and what we are today because our lives have always followed this predictable course.

If we want to develop new, more desirable types of behavior, the secret is to rearrange things inside us so that the desired behavior—the behavior that we have decided we want to change to—can be accomplished by following a new path of least resistance.

Imagine you'd like to build a house out in the middle of what is now a river. That can only be done if you have the ability to change the direction of the water flow—and move the river somewhere else! How do you do that? By changing the structure that forms the path of least resistance—which, in the case of a river, is the shape of the riverbed. All you have to do is restructure the riverbed, and you'll find that the water is perfectly willing to run in a completely different direction.

Or, let's imagine that we have a friend who would like to lose some weight but who loves fattening foods (particularly chocolate cake) too much to give them up.

Now, eating the chocolate cake at every opportunity is currently, for this person, the path of least resistance. He needs to change his belief structure in a way that creates a *new* path of least resistance, one that doesn't include chocolate cake.

And I'll help our friend do just that—with a fluffy, delicious chocolate cake, and a heavy rubber mallet.

I'll say to him, "Before we get started, how would you like to have a piece of this chocolate cake?"

He, of course, will look at the chocolate cake and decide to have some.

But once he grabs his fork, takes a big chunk of cake, and begins to savor his treat, I'll whack him on the head with the rubber mallet while he's still enjoying the first bite.

In a moment he'll get up off the floor, dazed and blinking, dust the cake crumbs off, and sit back down. Now, if this guy's a slow learner, he'll take another mouthful and get whacked again with the mallet! But let me assure you that this time when he manages to get up, sit back down, and clear his head, he's not going to be in the least bit interested in any more cake. If I offer him another piece, he'll throw up his hands and quickly say he's had all of the stuff he needs, thank you very much.

Now, does there seem to be a lot of self discipline or willpower involved here? No. This fellow's simply following *his new path of least resistance.* Because you see, it is now

56

easier for him to give up the cake than it is to get hit over the head again. His beliefs about what's desirable and undesirable about eating chocolate cake have changed—dramatically.

This is an example of someone radically changing his behavior by *simply making a new decision about priorities*. He went instantly from a person who was an absolute slave to the cake to someone who could turn it down with virtually no effort at all. That's how powerful our beliefs are.

But by now you're probably thinking, "Oh, come on...you've at least got to give me something believable to believe, and that example just isn't realistic. Nobody hits me over the head with a rubber mallet when I eat fattening foods."

Well, you're right about that; you don't get hit over the head. You just get fat, fatigued, and less likely to live a long, healthy life. You don't feel as good as you used to. But most important, you've lost a lot of self-esteem because deep down you know a major part of your life is out of control.

Frankly, I'd just as soon somebody would hit me over the head with a hammer and get it over with. At least then I'd have enough reason to stop this self destructive habit!

Create a False Bottom

If we had more adversity in our lives, we could find the strength to change ourselves into what we wish we could be. Adversity builds character. As Nietzche said, "That which doesn't kill me, strengthens me." But isn't it possible to find a way to build character *without* having to suffer? Why do we insist upon life dealing us miserable situations before we can find a way to grow?

Do you remember earlier on when I told you about the day I *decided* to be fed up with being fat? That was the beginning of the creation of a false, or artificial, bottom for me. After all, I can have all the mental and emotional benefits of hitting bottom right now if I can find a way to make where I am right now the bottom.

57

All I, or you, have to do is *decide that the present situation is no longer tolerable.* You might decide, for instance, that your temper is damaging your relationships, and that you need to gain more control of it. But this has to be a quality decision! And what I mean by that is, you must somehow arrive at a place in your life where you're ready to *genuinely* make the commitment.

It helps a lot if you clearly understand what's involved here. This is a choice for you between two evils. Every time you start to experience uncontrolled anger, you must choose either the seemingly unbearable effort it takes to control yourself and the suffering you will experience by hurting those you love with your bad temper.

In every case, it will be your true priority—what you've decided is most important to you—that determine which of the two alternatives is the lesser of the evils for you.

Once you understand this, it will become possible to exert a great deal of control over your entire belief system. It is important that you try to get used to the idea that you can *decide* what to believe; it really is *your* choice. Once you begin to clearly see the magnificence of this concept, it'll be much easier for you to make the decisions that produce statements like: "I cannot and will not continue to live my life this way. This will have to change." The price you're paying for your present self-defeating behavior can become too much to pay...as soon as you *decide* it is. When that happens, the pain will have exceeded the pleasure and you'll find a brand-new set of incentives to help you begin moving in a better direction. And the strength of these incentives, the amount of power they give you, will be directly dependent upon the quality of the new decision and your willingness to follow through long enough to install it completely.

Purposely Build Your Desire For Change

I've already told you that change is driven primarily by desire. The more you want it, the more likely it is that it will happen. In fact, if your desire to change a particular part of your life is strong enough, the change will be *easy* to make.

So, it's a pretty safe bet that if there's something in your life you haven't been able to accomplish, *you simply don't want it badly enough.* One of the real keys, then, to being able to make your dreams a reality is to learn the art of desire building.

We've all heard a story like this one. A man has been smoking his entire adult life. He really wants to quit but he hasn't been able to. His Lower Self thoroughly enjoys smoking and is hopelessly addicted to it. Of course another part of him, his Higher Self, knows smoking is bad for him, but in this case, his Lower Self is much stronger and is in control. But that can be changed...and here's how it might happen.

Let's say our friend goes to his doctor for an examination. The diagnosis is lung cancer. The doctor explains that the growth can be removed, but if the patient keeps smoking cigarettes he's going to die.

Now there's suddenly a very good chance that this man has smoked his last cigarette! The knowledge that smoking *will* kill him—now, this year—has tipped the balance. He now has enough evidence of the damage from his habit to increase his Higher Self's *desire* to stop. And, at that point, the Higher Self is able to take over, and, at last, a long-standing bad habit is abandoned.

Let me give you another example of desire building...one along more positive lines, the kind you can willfully choose to construct. As you will learn in a later lesson, I make it a practice to meditate every day because I think it's the single most powerful tool we have in our effort to gain control of ourselves. When I first learned about meditation, after reading only one book on the subject, I set out to install a daily meditation routine. In the beginning, I have to tell you, it was terribly boring and, contrary to what you probably think, hard work. And so after a couple of weeks of making myself meditate every day, I found some excuse one morning not to. Of course, the next morning I used the fact that I hadn't meditated the day before as an excuse not to do it then. Instead, I promised myself that I'd "start again Monday." But, of course, I didn't.

After a couple of months had gone by, I guess I forgot how hard it was and decided to try it again. This try also lasted only for a couple of weeks. In fact, I went through this scenario several times before I realized what needed to be done.

You see, my Lower Self wasn't the least bit interested in being alone, still, and silent for 30 minutes every morning. It's much too fidgety and it needs more stimulation than that. This was, of course, the part of me that thought meditation was boring.

But the real problem was that my Higher Self didn't have a strong enough desire for the benefits of meditation to overcome my Lower Self's opposition. So, I decided I would learn more about meditation. I knew that once I learned about its additional benefits, I would get more excited about meditating every day.

So I bought every book I could find on meditation and, sure enough, as I read I did become more and more excited about what the practice could do for me. Gosh, it turned out to be even better than I'd originally thought! As I read about what people had accomplished by using this powerful mental tool, my desire to give it another try got stronger and stronger. And when my desire became stronger than my Lower Self's objections, I began a daily meditation routine that has served me tremendously for a number of years.

But I couldn't have done it without *purposely building a desire for the end result.* If you can build a sufficient amount of desire to fuel your quest for change, you'll find yourself equipped with a brand-new sense of power. Your "willpower" will miraculously be much stronger, and this additional strength will allow you to decide to create a bottom in whatever part of your life you'd like to change.

So I find it's a good idea first to learn all you can about the benefits you'll receive as a result of making a life change. And you should become well acquainted, if you're not already, with all of the reasons you ought to give up the old behavior.

60

At this point, you'll be able to look at your situation in an entirely different way. A serious, well-thought-out decision to make some aspect of your life intolerable to you will change how you view everything. And if you continue to insist that the old behavior is now totally unacceptable and must be removed, big things will begin to happen.

But you have to *really* believe it. You must dedicate yourself to the principle that *you are in control of what you believe.* After all, you can decide to believe virtually anything (within reasonable boundaries, of course). And even if you don't convince yourself the first few times, if you'll keep insisting that this *is* your new belief and begin acting as if it is, you'll find out that your beliefs really can be altered. It may take a little time, depending on the level of emotional involvement (how strong your Lower Self is), but you can, indeed, change what you believe. And, you don't have to hit a real bottom to do it! Create a false bottom, find a new path of least resistance, increase your desire, and you'll find yourself with the ability to build a water-shed...anywhere you want one.

Life Lesson 7

Your Beliefs Create Your Reality

Your Perception of Life Is
Determined by What You Believe

I realize that's a rather profound statement. Nonetheless, it's true. Your beliefs do, in fact, have a dramatic effect on what you perceive to be reality. The common view, of course, is the exact opposite. Most people think that beliefs are based on their perception of the world around them. But since we all filter out a great deal of our environment (even though we may not be aware we're doing so) each of us experiences a different reality. In a very real sense, no two of us live in the same world. There are couples, for instance, who have been married for decades when something—maybe just an opinion voiced—makes them both realize that although they thought they shared everything, they have, in some ways, lived two very different lives.

I'd like to help you stretch your mind just a bit on this subject of reality...so let me tell you a little story.

Have You Heard About the New Amusement Park?

Forget for a moment about life as we know it here on Earth. Imagine that you and I are somewhere that does not look at all like Earth. In fact, it looks like—well, it looks like nothing. There is no planet, not even a solar system. You see, this story takes place in a nonphysical location. When it comes to the five senses, there just isn't anything here. Except that there *are* things here—and you and I are among them. We exist as personalities, as nonphysical beings, on a plane of pure consciousness. We maintain friendships and relationships with similar beings, and communicate through nonverbal methods.

Now, it seems that a friend of yours is all excited about something. He tells you—telepathically, of course—about something that's happening over on the other side of the universe.

"They call it an amusement park," he tells you.

"An amusement park? What's that?" you ask.

"Well, as far as I can tell it's a place that was built just for the purpose of having fun."

"Really?"

"Yeah, but it's rather strange. I understand they made it out of compressed localized energy fields that they call 'matter.'"

"What's that?"

"Look," he says, a little testily, "I don't know much more about it than you do. So would you just let me finish?"

"Okay, okay."

"All right then. Anyway, this matter is solid, which means it interacts in a physical way, primarily with other matter. Of course as nonmaterial beings, I don't think we'll really get the hang of it until we actually get there and see for ourselves."

"Of course," you say politely, not really following at all.

"Now the amusement park itself is in the shape of a huge ball—a 'planet' I believe is the term. And everything else is stuck to it by some force field called 'gravity.'"

"Gravity—?" you are about to ask, but catch yourself.

"They call the place 'Earth.'"

"Oh, 'Earth.'"

"Right," he continues. "Now, anyone can enter this amusement park, but you have to buy a ride ticket."

You can't help yourself. "What kinds of rides do they have?"

"I asked the same thing. It's up to you. You can buy any kind of ride you'd like. You can buy a long ride or a short one. It can be a smooth ride, an exciting ride, or a rough, bumpy ride."

"Why would anyone request a rough ride?"

"Well, apparently there are those who like to build in some challenge, you know, to make the ride more interesting. So they request problems to solve along the way. After all, games are not much fun if they're too easy to win."

64

"Let me get this straight," you interject. "I can have a fun ride or an easy ride or a problem-filled ride; it's all up to me."

"You got it."

"If we ride...what do we ride *in*?"

"That's another interesting thing about the place," says your friend. "You take the ride in a vehicle they call a 'body.'"

"Don't tell me, it's made of matter."

"Did someone tell you already?"

"No, lucky guess I suppose. Go ahead."

"Well, you're right. These 'bodies' are made of matter. They come in various sizes and colors, but the basic shape is a central cylinder with appendages, called 'arms' and 'legs,' for maneuvering around in the park. And they also come equipped with various senses to help you interact with your surroundings."

"What kind of senses?"

"Well, for instance, they have two little cameras mounted in the front so you can 'see' things in the park."

"Strange. What if I don't like the, ah, 'body' I get? Can I change my mind?"

"I'm not really sure. I know you get to choose, but once you make your selection I think your choices are somewhat limited."

"So how does the ride start?" you ask, really intrigued by now.

"Well, you just kind of slip into one of the, uh, bodies, and an operator sort of straps you in. Then they close the door on your little vehicle and you lose your memory."

"What?"

"That's right. You won't know where you are, where you came from, where you're going, or even what you're supposed to be doing."

"How do I find out?"

"Evidently these are questions you have to work out for yourself while you're taking the ride."

"So basically I get to decide for myself," you say.

"Yup. As far as I can make out, it's up to the individual. Of course, there will be other "people"—that's what they call a

65

body with one of us in it—at the amusement park when you arrive, so you'll discover some basic guidelines just by watching them. I suppose you can always just do what everyone else does."

"So what you're saying is that it's all up to me: what kind of ride I have, figuring out who—or what—I am, and what I'm supposed to be doing."

"Yep. That's about the size of it. Then, when your time is up, the ride ends—usually as abruptly as it started. Your vehicle wears out, breaks down, or, I guess, just quits. It refuses to work anymore. At that point the attendant opens the door, lets you out, and says, "Well, how did you like your ride?"

What Do You Think?

Now let me ask you: If you truly believed that you were actually just a personality with no physical body, and that you were only taking a ride in an amusement park—an experience that couldn't hurt you—would you look at things differently? Would you go through this life with a little more gusto? Would you take yourself less seriously? And would the things that seem so important to you now remain that way?

If you were convinced that you were a spiritual being only here to have a short diversion from your real life, wouldn't you experience this life in a totally different way? Of course you would!

If you were convinced that your life here was just for fun and didn't really matter, your values and priorities—the way you live your whole life—would be dramatically different. That's because your beliefs have a huge impact on how you perceive reality and different life situations. But let me give you a couple of true-to-life examples.

I once owned a motor home, for a short while, as a result of a real estate trade. Now, it just so happened that Ted Moran, an old Navy buddy of mine visited me during the brief time it sat in my driveway. Somehow we got the idea to go on a little tour of

66

what was then my home state of New Mexico, and so we packed up late one evening and headed for Santa Fe.

I got tired that night and Ted volunteered to drive the rest of the way while I slept.

I issued some last-minute instructions before I went to sleep, telling him that there would be a lot of beautiful wooded places around Santa Fe for a campsite, and that he could just pick any one he liked. With that, I dozed off, and didn't wake up until the next morning.

Well, when I woke up I was really feeling what I call "campy." You know, that special feeling you get just by being out and about in the woods. Ted was already up and busy filling the motor home with the mouthwatering smell of bacon and eggs.

While he finished cooking breakfast, I grabbed a quick shower. I shaved, combed my hair, threw on a pair of jeans, and decided to get myself a nice deep whiff of pine tree and wildflower air. "Wow!" I thought to myself. "There's nothing like being out in the woods cooking breakfast!"

I swung open the door and stuck my head out, all ready to fill my lungs with that fresh mountain air, when I saw that *we were parked in the middle of the parking lot of the biggest shopping center in Santa Fe!*

Wow, what a shock! Let me assure you that from that moment on, the inside of that motor home was a much different place to be. I no longer felt campy and woodsy—I felt like an idiot!

What's also interesting about that experience is that I could have had that dramatic shift in my perspective even if my friend had just *told* me where we were rather than me having to open the door and see for myself.

If he'd just said, "By the way, Joe, the only place I could find to park last night was in the middle of this great big shopping center," I would, at that point, have radically changed my beliefs about what was going on here. And although nothing inside the motor home would have changed, I would have then seen my situation in a totally different way. A brand new reality.

Let me give you another example of a large shift in perspective that resulted from a change in beliefs.

One of my best friends lives in Southern California. His name is Hal Morris. Hal told me about an experience that I think is one of the best examples I've ever heard.

It seems that he and his wife, Connie, were touring the Ronald Reagan Presidential Library on the day of its opening. The tour took a couple of hours and they thoroughly enjoyed it. Hal's a pretty staunch Republican, and he felt it was an honor to be there.

He told me, for instance, that the re-creation of the Reagan Oval Office was awesome. He went on to tell me how beautiful the entire facility was—that it was decorated with such wonderful taste and style.

But on their way out, he looked down from a second story walkway and spotted an ugly piece of modern art standing next to a wall. It was an odd-shaped carving, made of stone, with edges that were jagged and rough. It had what appeared to be graffiti-like writing on the side of it. Now Hal couldn't believe that whoever had so tastefully decorated this very conservative and traditional tribute to one of our presidents had chosen to use that unseemly piece of modern art, out in the middle of everything. It was so out of place!

He was still scoffing as they headed down the stairs to the ground level to leave.

Now, it so happened that this "statue thing" was right on the way to the exit, and when my friend walked past it he got a closer look. That's when he saw the plaque...the one that announced this was a piece of the stone that was taken from the place where Ronald Reagan put his hand on the Berlin Wall and said, "This wall must come down."

In an instant, Hal's attitude changed from one of contempt to one of awe and reverence. He realized, breathlessly, that this wasn't a piece of modern art, this was a piece of *history,* and an awesome one at that. He said he stood before that old piece of stone with goosebumps as he thought about what it represented and what a truly profound place it commanded in the history of the world.

Of course, nothing had changed about that stone...except Hal Morris's belief about what it was. But when he changed his *belief,* his reality also changed. At that point the object was magically transformed, at least for him, from something to be made fun of to a treasure to be regarded with great respect.

And your entire life, your reality, could change *just as dramatically*...if you simply found a way to change your beliefs about what's going on here and the part you play in it.

What You Believe Is Up to You

There are two overriding rules about believing that I call the two principles of human belief. We all innately know these rules, but most of us have not stopped long enough to consider how we can make them work for us. They are:

1. You are solely in charge of what you believe.
2. You can believe *anything* as long as it can't be disproved.

Let's take them one at a time. Rule number one cannot be circumvented. No matter how much money you have or how many people you have serving you, no one will ever be able to take over the responsibility of choosing your beliefs. There's no one person who is authorized to come up with what you're going to believe. Forming a belief is an *individual* human function and every one of us has an equal right to do it. In other words, you're just as capable of deciding what to believe as anyone is. Oh, you may choose to adopt someone else's beliefs, but *you* will have made that decision. No one can decide your beliefs but you.

Unfortunately, most people settle for adopting the most popular beliefs of the society in which they happen to live...and then they wonder why they can't seem to break out of the pack and make their lives as successful as they want them to be! But your life—from your thoughts to your circumstances—is a result of what *you* believe. So if you didn't purposely choose your basic core beliefs, you've got some work to do. Since you unconsciously chose the beliefs that have created your life up until this point, you are now perfectly capable of consciously abandoning some of them and re-choosing beliefs that will serve instead of defeat you.

Rule number two requires a little more explanation. Because, unfortunately, most people, at least at first blush, don't agree with it. Let's look at it once more.

*You can believe anything as long as **it can't be disproved.***

Have you ever heard the term "your guess is as good as mine?" Well, believe it or not, as unimportant as that old cliche may sound, it's one of the more profound governing principles of our lives. We apply that little phrase anytime we can't *know* the truth of a matter. What's on the other side of the known universe? Beats me—your guess is as good as mine. See how it works? In other words, if there's something that we *can't* know, we get to fill in the blanks with a guess...or to use a more appropriate word, by adopting a *belief.*

But could any question be important enough to force us to *make up an answer*? Absolutely. Let me give you five of them. What am I? Where am I? Where did I come from? Where am I going? Why do I exist?

I think you'll have to admit that those are pretty heavy questions. In fact, they are so important that we *must* have answers to them in order to enjoy any emotional stability or peace of mind. You just can't lead a meaningful, worthwhile life if they are left totally unanswered. Let's face it, no one's going to be able to give you *the* answers. These things are clearly *unknowable.* And what you choose to believe about them is up to you.

We have a whole world full of people, for instance, who think *their* religion is the one true religion. They feel really sorry for the rest of humanity, who missed the truth—those who came to a different conclusion about what to believe than they did. And they all have a perfect right to believe this, because there's no way to prove their opinions are right or wrong.

Of course there are people whose faith is so strong that they mistake their beliefs for knowledge. Let me address that issue quickly in case you are one of those people.

First of all, let me say that I have an enormous amount of respect for anyone with that kind of faith. You are so secure in your religious beliefs that you feel you *know* the truth and that puts you among the most fortunate people around. But let me point out to you that what we're really talking about is *faith*. Christians, for instance, are told in the New Testament that without faith you can't please God (Heb. 11:6). You see, if you *knew* the truth you wouldn't *need* any faith because faith, by its very definition, is a belief in something that is not known. And so although I heartily applaud the depth of your convictions, I must point out that the truth of spiritual matters cannot be known and therefore must be believed.

But on the other hand, there are some things that we don't have a right to believe: you can't believe something that can be disproved. If, for instance, you and I were sitting at an outdoor restaurant at noon, I would sound pretty silly telling you that I believed the sun wasn't shining—that it was dark outside. All you have to do is point to the sun, because it's obvious to both of us that it's the middle of the day. It makes no sense for me to believe it's dark outside, because it's *known* that it's not. But at that same time I could say, "Something really good is going to happen to me tomorrow," and you couldn't disprove my statement at that time and place. Why? Because it deals with the future, and the future is *unknown* to us.

You see, I have a perfect right to believe that something great is going to happen to me tomorrow. Of course, I also have the right to believe that tomorrow will be a terrible day and that misfortune will come my way. And it all boils down to the fact that these beliefs can't be proven wrong because they're unknown.

71

Now just in case you're saying to yourself, "Does he mean that I ought to just make beliefs up about those things that can't be proven and just decide to believe them...because I want to?" Let me give you my answer: a resounding yes. *That's precisely what I'm saying.* And this idea really isn't a new one. In fact, it's not only accepted, it's respected.

Do you remember when Magic Johnson made the announcement that he was infected with the HIV virus? The next words out of his mouth were something to the effect of, "But don't worry about me, because I'm going to lead a long and productive life." Now isn't that interesting? How do you suppose he knew he was going to live a long life? He didn't. He couldn't have. Then why did he make that statement? Because he *believes* it. And why does he hold that belief? Because he decided that he could have a much better life if he chose to believe it and conducted his inner life accordingly.

You may see this concept as being as simple as "looking on the bright side." Although that's correct, it goes much deeper than that.

Which One of You Makes Your Decisions?
When you take all the window dressing off, the most basic decision any of us ever makes is which of our two selves will be in charge of the ongoing decision making process. We must decide which self is going to establish the basic beliefs, priorities, and behavior patterns that will serve as the foundation for our lives. Will you continue to allow a large part of your life to be controlled by your Lower Self, basing your decisions entirely on emotions? Or will you find a way to move the process over to your Higher Self, and make those decisions out of better judgment?

You see, Magic Johnson had precisely that choice to make. When he learned he had a potentially deadly virus, he had to make a decision about how to view his situation and what effect it would have on his sense of well-being. Apparently he was smart enough to realize, as we all should, that every moment

72

spent worrying about the future robs us of that which is most important to us today. And so he stepped into his Higher Self and made the decision about his future from better judgment instead of emotion.

We know that if he had turned the decision about how to feel about his circumstances over to his Lower Self, he would have gotten an emotional reaction. Now let me ask you, if you faced that kind of situation and then looked to your emotions for a way to respond, what would you get? Fear, of course. It's the appropriate emotion for this kind of news. And so that's a great time to stay out of your Lower Self and get firmly planted in your Higher Self.

Decisions like these made from the Lower Self result in a loss of control. Once we become fearful, the fear becomes our mind-set and of course the resulting state of mind brings us a stressful, unstable, and very uncomfortable condition.

But because Magic Johnson realized that he could be emotionally stable and happy if he believed that somehow, in spite of the virus, he would lead a long and healthy life...he decided to believe that very thing!

This is a perfect example of someone taking direct control of his belief systems and purposely choosing a belief that would best serve him. Wouldn't it be much better if we had the opportunity to consciously *decide* what our beliefs would be? After all, if you can't know, you ought to be able to choose to believe that which benefits you the most. If you have to believe something, why not choose to believe in a way that lays an emotional foundation that will allow you to live your life the way you'd like to...with peace and courage and honor? You can if you know how.

It's in your best interest to hold beliefs that will comfort, satisfy, and sustain you through the tough times. What you will wind up with, of course, is faith. The New Testament defines faith as "the substance of things hoped for, the evidence of things not seen" (Hebrews 11:1). And we can define fear, faith's direct opposite, by changing a single word of that

73

definition. Fear is "the substance of things hoped *against*, the evidence of things not seen."

We're talking about things that haven't happened yet. It's anybody's guess how they'll turn out. We either have fear that something bad will happen or faith that something good will happen. But you'll never have them both at the same time, and you get to choose which one you want!

Life Lesson 8

It's Up To You To Decide What Life Is All About

It was the summer of 1989. I had just sold my companies and put all the assets I could find into passive investments that would provide me all the income I needed. Then, with my life basically on automatic pilot, I spent a lot of time in what I suppose you could call seclusion. It wasn't that I wanted to be antisocial, I was just very busy with a pressing new project and I didn't have time for anything else.

You see, for the first time in my adult life I didn't have a dream. Up until then, I had lived to make money. My goal of becoming a multimillionaire had consumed the last twenty five years of my life. But, when I found myself retired from business, I was forty four years old...and I had no idea who I was. I woke up every morning and asked myself the same questions over and over. Do I have a goal? What am I interested in? And, of course, the big one: Is there something I'm supposed to be doing?

I don't think I've ever had a more empty feeling than I did during those first few weeks after my retirement. My old motivations and goals had vanished. I just wasn't interested in making money anymore. Someone once said that money is like sex, it's only important when you don't have any. Well, I had more money than I could spend, and the idea of making more of it just didn't interest me at all. Only one thing was clear: It was time for me to move on to phase two of my life...if I could just figure out what that was.

Luckily, by then I understood the power of my beliefs.

The Big Picture

Most people think if you can't find something with the five senses, it doesn't exist. But that's a big mistake. Our refusal to

75

believe anything we can't physically verify keeps our thinking too small. If we're going to try to make sense of all of all this—to provide ourselves with answers about the nature of and reason for our existence—we're going to have to break free of the bonds of our physical senses.

If it sounds to you like we're getting into a discussion of spirituality, you're right— that's precisely the next subject we're going to talk about. But before we do, let's take a moment and decide exactly what we want the word "spirituality" to mean, because I'm amazed that so few people even consider the possibility that spirituality extends beyond religion. Indeed, most of us do confine our ideas of spirituality to the concepts we've learned in our own religious practice and never consider that it might go further. But spirituality is larger than just our religious beliefs. In fact, the word spirituality should include *everything* that exists which can't be perceived with our five senses, including the real essence of our own inner being.

I define spirituality, then, simply as *nonphysical reality*. If something exists, but we can't detect it with any of our five senses, it falls within what I define as the spiritual realm.

After all, logic would tell us that there has to be a lot more going on than meets the eye. There simply are not enough answers available to us in the physical arena—there must be something more.

The folks at the cutting edge of science—those involved in trying to understand quantum physics—will tell you that science is no longer sure what physical reality is. The solid substances we call matter now appear to be made from nonmatter—from energy fields that are apparently aligned in a way that makes physical objects *seem* solid. But the very same ingredients that make up a tree also make up the seemingly empty space next to the tree. It would seem that this minuscule building block (whatever it is) can be arranged in a way so as *not* to appear solid when that is the desired effect.

There are even quantum physicists—quite respected folks, mind you—who claim that there's a strong possibility that the final construction of matter takes place *within our minds* as we

76

interpret the stimuli we receive from our five senses. In other words, unless somebody looks at it...it isn't there!

Now it's not my intent to teach you about quantum physics (not that I could if I wanted to). But if we're going to increase our perception of reality in order to see a bigger picture, we must loosen up our imagination and learn to believe in things we can't see (not to mention, hear, touch, smell, or taste).

One of the biggest steps you can take toward expanding your awareness of reality is to stop depending on your five senses as your only means of determining what is real. A lack of physical evidence should never keep us from exploring any possibility.

What Are We...Really?

According to polls, the overwhelming majority of us believe that we will, in some form, transcend physical death. Now, if you believe that some unseen and totally undetectable part of you will leave your body at the time of physical death, that part of you would fall squarely into our definition of the spiritual: It's real, it exists, it even lives, but it's certainly not physical. So, I'll refer to this part of us as our spirit.

Of course, we don't know much about our spirit. No scientist has ever been able to pinpoint the "secret of life" that makes the difference between a living body and a lifeless pile of natural elements. No one knows what makes our brain into a conscious, thinking lump of physical matter. But, just the same, our spirit—that undetectable part of us that leaves our body and continues to exist after we "die"—is very much a real part of us. Your spirit is as real as your right hand. And the fact that you can't see it or feel it doesn't make it any less so.

It seems to me that the time has come for all of us, whether we're "religious" or not, to accept the fact that we not only have a spirit within us, but in reality we *are* that spirit—it is our true identity.

Let me see if I can't give you a little piece of logic that I think will prove to you—based on your own present beliefs— that your spirit is the real you. If you believe you somehow

77

existed before your physical birth, or that you will continue to exist and live on in some other form after your death, then doesn't it make sense to you that your physical body is the temporary part of you and that the part that preceded your birth and will continue to exist after your death is the *real* you?

To paraphrase what Dr. Wayne Dyer says so aptly in his wonderful book *Real Magic*, *we are not physical beings attempting to have a temporary spiritual experience, we are spiritual beings having a temporary physical experience.*

The shift that occurs when you take this viewpoint gives you a much bigger picture of reality—a reality that is filled with unlimited possibilities. Of course, the majority of us, to some degree, have already become convinced of the existence of a spiritual realm. Without this belief we wouldn't have anything to base our religious beliefs on. But we need to make this unseen part of existence more real by giving it the importance it deserves. We must be aware that there are things we can't see that are much more important than anything we can. But mainly we need to realize that we're not from here...we belong somewhere else.

Then Why Did We Come Here?

That's a very good question. In fact, I spent most of the latter part of 1989 trying to find an answer for it.

Being a logical person, I decided to approach the problem with logic and see how far that would take me. I was looking for a new purpose for my life and although I wanted to be able to consider as large a picture of reality as possible, the belief I ended up with also needed to make sense. My new beliefs would certainly have to fit with what I knew to be true in my physical life.

To begin with, it just made sense to me that I'd be foolish to dedicate the rest of my life to something I wouldn't be able to take with me when it was over. If I am a spiritual being from a cosmic plane somewhere, why would I want to come to this planet, suffer the limitations of being housed in this body, and spend my entire life building a pile of something I'll just have to wave good-bye to when I leave? So I decided that I would eliminate from my list of possible things to dedicate my life to anything that wouldn't survive my physical existence. That, of course, brought about a rather large round of wholesale elimination. In fact, I had to eliminate virtually everything that had, in the past, been important to me.

That's when I came to the realization that the only thing I'm going to be able to take with me when I leave this life is who and what I become while I'm here. So I must be here to undergo some kind of change. This life is a training ground! That's the only rational answer I could find.

You see, I've come to believe that we're living this life solely for the *experience*. Apparently, our physical existence somehow gives us a unique opportunity to grow and develop. Not knowing much about the spiritual realm, I couldn't even venture a guess as to what it is that we can accomplish here that we couldn't do there. But it must be something, or we'd still be there.

When I became convinced that this life is a school, seeing every event in my life as a lesson and every person as a teacher, my reality changed in profound ways that I couldn't have predicted.

I began to see all of the occurrences in my life in a much different light. Instead of making the things that happened and the circumstances they created my primary focus, I became more interested in what I could *learn* from those events and how I might benefit and grow as a result of having experienced them. This radical change in the way I saw life was simply a by-product of my decision to believe that what happens to me isn't nearly as important as what I *become* as a result of what happens to me.

When adversity came my way, instead of complaining and wondering why life was so unfair, I started looking for the lesson I could learn from it. As a result, I've discovered that adversity is a tremendous teacher. It not only provides us with important lessons, it has the unique ability to take us emotionally

79

to a place where we can accept and truly benefit from those lessons.

Your perception of what's important will change dramatically, too, when you realize, for example, that the next time you do something new that scares you, the actual circumstances of that situation won't be nearly as important as the courage you'll find to face your fear. Because that additional courage will become a part of you and will remain with you long after the circumstances that brought it about have been forgotten.

The next crisis you and your spouse go through won't be nearly as important as what happens to your relationship in the heat of that crisis. The alterations you make to the relationship will be there long after the crisis is over and has long since become an unimportant part of the past.

You'll lead a totally different life when you take a new view of what's important and make the events in your life *lessons* that give you the opportunity to do what you came here for—to grow, mature, learn, and develop into a better you.

Don't you wish your kids would take this approach to life? It might work like this; One of your children does something wrong and you find the need to discipline him. Afterwards, you notice that he's standing off in a corner, mumbling. Overcome with curiosity, you sneak up behind him, just close enough to hear.

Now get this. Instead of saying, "Mommy and daddy are so mean to me," or "Life's just not fair," he's asking himself a very good question: "How can I keep that from happening to me again?" Boy, wouldn't you love to have a son or daughter with that kind of attitude? This kid is ready, willing, and able to gain from life everything it has to offer. And all he has to do to arm himself with this tremendous advantage is to look past the adversities and use them as an opportunity to become a little wiser so he can make his life better in the future.

That's exactly what happens to us when we purposely live our lives in a way that reflects the belief that life is a school and that finding a way to benefit from the things that happen to us is much more important than the fact that they did happen.

But Who's Running This School?

If I'm going to believe that this earth is a school and that I've been sent here for the purpose of growth, I have to abandon the idea that anything "just happens". To tell you the truth, I didn't much like the idea of living in a universe where things just happen, anyway. The cosmos is much too big for me to control, so I'd rather someone else had a firm grip on the wheel. *Someone* has to be in charge.

Now I'm certainly not a preacher; nor do I have any particular religious agenda I'm interested in getting you to believe or follow. My own religious beliefs are very important to me, but I'm of the opinion that forming these kinds of beliefs is a very personal matter and that everyone has the ability to come to his or her own conclusions.

So I will generally be using the term "higher power," because I know that people from virtually every religious persuasion will read this book. Alcoholics Anonymous refers to this generic concept of God as "your higher power, whatever you perceive that to be." I'm comfortable with that. I'm not telling you who God is or what He wants. I am, instead, telling you that there isn't much chance of having peace of mind, courage, or comfort in your life unless you have a belief in and a reliance on a higher power.

There also is only one way to be comfortable in the knowledge that a greater power is in charge and that that power loves you and is protecting you. And that way is to simply choose a belief that provides you with this kind of comfort and understanding and dedicate yourself to believing it.

You see, lightning probably isn't going to strike in a way that will somehow magically give you all of the answers to your spiritual questions. Faith is a matter of believing and you are solely in charge of your beliefs. So, stop waiting for something to come along and convince you that your higher power is taking care of you. There is nothing wrong with *deciding* to believe it...and when you do, the result can be almost as powerful as if lightning did strike.

In case you're misunderstanding me, let me clearly say that I'm not advocating that you just "grab" something and decide to believe it. It obviously has to be something that is believable to you. What I'm saying is, if you find a particular religion or person of God who holds a set of religious beliefs that strike you as being the truth, why not fully and purposefully embrace these principles, rather than believing in them halfheartedly...waiting to be further convinced? It certainly seems to me that we'd be much better off deciding to become enthusiastic believers of something instead of waiting on some additional "proof" from God to totally convince us.

So what I *decided* was that I would purposely trust a higher power to know and do what was best. I decided to believe wholeheartedly that my higher power loves, protects, and cares for me in ways I can't even imagine.

You see, it's one thing to sit around and *hope* that there is a higher power on your side, and it's quite another to make a conscious decision to *believe* that your higher power loves you and *is* continually assisting and protecting you. I've stopped asking for any further proof of God's existence. I realized that it was up to me to generate my own faith. So now I'm *depending* on things now that, in the past, I had only *hoped* were real. I had professed a belief in God for years, but when I realized that I was in charge of my beliefs, I made a much deeper commitment to totally trust my higher power, and my faith has grown tremendously as a result.

Everyone has the ability to find his or her God, just as I did. And although it makes no difference to me *what* you believe, your beliefs make a tremendous difference to *you*. I don't think I've ever met anyone who actively, honestly, and sincerely sought to find and establish a relationship with his or her higher power who didn't succeed. We can plainly see that people who have formed meaningful relationships with a higher power lead much more meaningful and confident lives. The process of believing is an inward one. You can go gather all the advice you want to, but in the end the decision will be yours. And when you do arrive at a sincere, honest understanding with your higher power and find yourself at peace with that arrangement, you'll have filled a huge void deep within you with comfort, assurance, and security.

Believing in the "Greater Good"

An important part of my belief in a higher power is the conviction that there are no random occurrences. Nothing just happens. Instead, I've chosen to believe that everything that occurs in my life happens for a reason and will contribute to what I call the greater good. In other words, everything happens for my benefit: I am convinced that if it did happen, it *needed* to happen.

When I decided to believe in the idea that everything contributes to the greater good, my confidence increased dramatically. You see, confidence is your faith in your ability to meet and master the problems you'll face in the future. Because we can't know what the future will bring, we must find a way to become convinced that we can *handle* whatever it brings. Of course, there's no way I can *know* I'll be up to the job of mastering whatever comes my way in the unknown future, so I must...*believe* it.

In studying the major religions of the world, I've noticed something really interesting. There is a group of what I call universal concepts. These are the beliefs that are contained in most, if not all, of them. The belief that people have universally used throughout history to give themselves the confidence necessary to live life boldly and with purpose is the commonly-held belief that "God will never allow more adversity to come upon me than I can bear." Well, that pretty well solves the problem! There are literally millions of people who believe that, and when they do, it provides them with a tremendous amount of comfort and confidence. These people can live life as an adventure.

We all like adventure...at least under certain circumstances. Most of us, for instance, really enjoy an action-packed adventure movie. You know the kind I mean: The hero and the heroine have a mission to accomplish but their path is fraught with danger. Every now and then, it looks like they're doomed—but they always find a way at the last moment to escape and continue their quest.

Do you know why we all enjoy action adventure movies so much? It's because deep down, during the entire film, we know that everything is going to turn out all right in the end. They're not going to die...we all know that. And when you think everything's going to turn out all right, the more dangerous and threatening situations there are, the more fun it is!

Of course taking chances isn't nearly as much fun in real life for most of us. You see, if we don't believe that things will turn out all right for us, our fears will keep us from any attempt at boldness.

So what we all need is a profound, deep-rooted belief that everything's going to be okay. That's why I have chosen to believe in the greater good. And when we truly believe in this magnificent concept, we can live our lives as an adventure, eagerly looking forward to every new twist and turn.

It's All Up to You

Let me make it clear once again that I'm not trying to tell you what you should believe. I only want to convince you that you can take control of those beliefs and make them whatever you want them to be. I've alluded to my core beliefs only to give you an example of a way to believe that provides the kinds of benefits we can receive from taking control of our belief system. If some or all of my beliefs have a ring of truth about them, feel free to use them. Or, now that you have the idea, you may prefer to formulate your own. It's entirely up to you.

I can't tell you what a tremendous difference this deliberate dedication to my spiritual beliefs has made in virtually every aspect of my life. And I have to tell you that my new perspective also allows me to see these same principles working in other people's lives as well.

I remember one time when I was sharing the platform at a convention with several other speakers. A friend, who was scheduled to speak just before me, always made it a practice to tape a one hundred dollar bill under two or three of the seats in the meeting room before the audience arrived. Then, at a point during his speech, he'd ask everyone to feel underneath their chairs. Of course, there's always a great rumbling throughout the audience and pretty soon the cheers that come from two or three areas of the room confirm that the money has been found. Then, as soon as everything settles down and everyone is seated again, he makes his point. He tells the lucky ones, as they continue to shake hands with those around them and happily wave their hundred dollar bills, that good things can happen...when you least expect them.

Well, at that particular event, he had given his speech, complete with the money discovery exercise, and then the audience had been given a short break. As they were starting to mill back into the room, I went up front, ready to give my speech, and was greeted by one of the convention officials.

I asked him how things were going, and he looked at me and said, "You won't believe what happened just before the last speech." He told me that his boss had put him in charge of a couple of rows of chairs at the front of the meeting room that were designated as a VIP section. It seems that he had the unenviable task of telling people who came along that they couldn't sit in those chairs.

Once he had explained all this, he said: "A young guy walked over when I wasn't looking and sat down in the very first row of the VIP section. When I saw him sitting there"—and here he grimaced—"I went over and, as tactfully as I could, told him he'd have to move. I think it embarrassed him, but he kept a good attitude. He gave me kind of a timid smile, then he got up and moved over to the next section, found an empty seat, and sat down."

"Yeah?" I said, wondering why he was telling me this.

85

Then a big grin came onto to his face and he said, "Well, it just so happens that this time the kid sat down in one of the chairs that had a hundred dollar bill taped to the bottom of it!"

Well, needless to say, I thought it was a wonderful story. In fact, I relayed it to the audience that day during my speech, and when I did, I asked the young man to stand and be recognized. After the audience gave him an enthusiastic round of applause, I told him that he'd just had an opportunity to learn one of life's most important lessons: that the right attitude can, in unexpected ways, cause us to be exactly where we need to be, even if it doesn't seem that way at the time.

"You had a choice," I said. "You could have gotten really upset. You could have argued that you paid good money to be here and should be able to sit wherever you want. In fact, young man, you could have chewed everybody out and then stormed right out of here in a huff...and never known that your pride had cost you a hundred dollars."

In other words, who knows what's *really* supposed to happen! Do you really think with your little individual view of reality you're equipped to make a judgment like that? But a person who trusts that everything happens for a reason and that the greater good is always served, no matter how it appears at the time, not only leads a more peaceful life, but also often finds himself in the right place at the right time to receive serendipitous blessings that come from the most unexpected places. At least it *can* work that way—if you believe it does, and then expect it to.

What About Our Free Will?

A question I get asked regularly is, "How can you believe that a higher power will make things turn out in a certain way when we have the ability to choose a different course?"

Well, obviously we have been given the gift of free choice. It has to be that way in order for our school to operate effectively. The school we call life is different from any other school in that we only have to take the lessons we *need.* We sign up for our subjects by demonstrating to the universe that we have a deficiency in that area. In other words, we learn by making mistakes.

The idea of everything unfolding according to a plan will mix easily with the concept of free will if you see a big enough picture. Do you remember those little maze puzzles you used to work your way through with a pencil when you were a kid? There was only one entrance, but once you got in you had all kinds of choices about which way to go. Of course, most of them turned out to be dead ends, and so you turned around and tried some other path. Now if you were real smart, you could zip right through one of those things, but if you took many wrong turns, it could take a long time to find your way out.

Let me point out to you that in spite of all those choices in the middle, there was only one exit! You were destined to end up in that one place no matter how many wrong decisions you made along the way trying to figure out how to get there. While you were working the puzzle, your destiny was to reach that one place—a mission that could be accomplished in a thousand different ways. And the only way you could have failed in your mission was to stop trying before you got there.

That's the way I see life. We have the illusion that we can make choices that have a dramatic effect. To a degree, of course, that's very true. But if you look at a big enough picture you see that our decision making is nothing more than the trial-and-error process that allows us to learn and grow.

Only You Can Answer the Big Question

Since the beginning of recorded history, the human race has spent a lot of time wondering, "What is life all about?" Well, who'd have thought that, in the end, the responsibility of answering that question would be up to...you! Oh, I suppose it would be much easier if there were a nice, pat answer that everyone could use, but I think it's pretty obvious that this life just doesn't work that way. Like those folks taking their ride in the amusement park, we each decide, at least for us, what this life is all about. And as soon as you make that decision, you will have created your own unique reality. Life can be a series of chaotic events, randomly playing themselves out, or a perfect plan designed and conducted just for your benefit. It really is up to you...because when you decide to believe it, you will make it so.

Life Lesson 9

You Are Who You Think You Are

None of your beliefs have a greater impact on your life than the beliefs you have about yourself. The opinions you hold about your value or worth affect you more than you could possibly realize. The phrase "self-image" has been used for a long time to identify the feelings we have about our own worth. Admittedly, it's a well-worn and overused term and a lot of people have grown tired of it, but that doesn't make it any less valid or any less important.

In addition to being vital to your emotional well-being, your self-image dramatically affects your ability to accomplish your goals and fulfill your dreams for the future. It's very important that you become more aware of the way you feel about yourself and, just as important, where those feelings come from. You see, you'll never be able to really enjoy life, no matter what it offers, if you don't like or respect yourself.

Most people haven't given much thought to the necessity of self-esteem, so they try to find happiness outside themselves. But even the grandest of circumstances will not bring happiness to any of us if we don't feel good about who we are.

Believe it or not, people go to prison for the same reason *we* find ourselves in *our* circumstances. It's a result of their quest for happiness. They use drugs in an effort to make their lives more pleasurable or they steal from others to get enough money to "enjoy the good life." Unfortunately, these folks are busy committing all these crimes, not realizing that the very activity they are counting on to bring them happiness will rob them of the self-respect necessary to experience it.

I've had prison inmates tell me of fabulous riches and luxurious lifestyles they lived as the result of their criminal activities. But most of them, in moments of honesty, will admit that they were never really happy. There was always something missing. It was, of course, that they didn't feel good about themselves. They had no self-respect.

Let me see if I can't show you why self-image is so important. Imagine, if you will, that your only car is a 1953 Volkswagen Beetle—one that's been around the block a few too many times. Its left rear fender is crumpled beyond recognition. The exhaust pipe and one side of the front bumper drag on the ground. One headlight is broken and the other dangles in the breeze, suspended from its wires, as the car chugs along. The windshield is shattered and the headliner is torn and drooping so much that it rests on top of your head as you drive.

Now that you have a good picture of your automobile, imagine a little more for me. Pretend that you're about to take a vacation in that car to the most fabulous vacation spots in the country. Oh, and one more thing. For the entire duration of your trip, you must stay *inside* the car.

I think it's a safe bet that this is one vacation you're not even going to come close to enjoying. No matter which wonderful, scenic place you choose to visit, the beauty of it will be overridden by the feelings you get from being trapped in that old, broken down Bug. You see, your environment won't be the vacation spot as much as it will be the inside of the car—that's where you'll be. In the same light, you don't really live in your hometown. Instead, you actually live *inside yourself.* And you are never able to leave the environment you create for yourself in yourself.

So if you hold a low opinion of yourself, it will keep you from fully enjoying accomplishments, wealth, and relationships (*especially* relationships). You see, your assessment of yourself will always be a major factor in determining how much you get out of life and how enjoyable the experience will be.

Now, imagine that instead of having to drive the old, broken down Volkswagen, you have just been handed the keys to a brand new Ferrari. As you get into that sleek little job and crank the engine, you know you're going to have a great time, even if you're in the most desolate part of the Sahara Desert. That's because your outside circumstances always take a backseat to how you feel about yourself. You never get away from you. You must always be there, constantly reminding yourself of who you are.

Of course, the ideal situation in life is to drive the Ferrari *and* go to the wonderful vacation spots. Then, you'd not only have something to enjoy, you'd have the ability to enjoy it. Let's see if we can't figure out how to do that.

Building a Better Self-Image

Have you ever stopped to think about how much you're worth and why? You see, worth is the factor you use to determine how *worthy* you are to have the kind of life you want.

As I teach seminars in correctional facilities and talk with the inmates, I have become convinced that we could go a long way toward solving our nation's prison problem if criminals had the ability to formulate beliefs that would allow them to feel that they are of genuine value. Low self-image, or lack of self-esteem, is a severely debilitating condition that keeps them from even believing that they're worth the effort it would take to improve their lives. It's pretty clear to me that the overriding feeling among these people is one of inferiority and lack of worth. Oh, they try very hard to feel and act like they're important, but for the most part, they just don't get the job done.

If they found a set of beliefs that could genuinely convince them they have as much value or worth as any other human being, their life will start reflecting those beliefs.

And this is because all of us act in accordance with the standards we decide are appropriate for us. The process is pretty simple: low self-esteem...low standards. And unless we genuinely feel that we have value and worth as human beings, we'll never dedicate ourselves to any noble purpose—we'll always find ourselves, instead, acting in a way that reflects our low opinions of ourselves.

So, among the most important things you can do as you begin to rearrange your belief system is to find a belief that allows you to realize how much you're worth and what place you occupy in the grand scheme of the universe. The more valuable you can feel, the more quality you'll have in your life. *And that quality will reflect in everything you say, think, or do.* It's very simple: Quality can only be added to a person's life when that person feels worthy to live in a way that reflects quality.

For a long time I myself had a horrible self-image. In fact, I'm convinced that the real reason I dropped out of school at 16 was that I felt inferior to the other students—totally unable to compete with them. My lack of self-esteem also was a major contributor to my terrible attitude toward life back then. Without realizing it, I was always trying to compensate for those feelings of unworthiness and lack of value.

I found, though, that when I decided to form different beliefs about myself, my self-image really did improve. As I began replacing old habits, I felt more and more that I was worth the effort it took to make the next improvement. Then, the whole thing began to snowball. Each step I made toward becoming a better person brought with it a higher sense of worth, and that gave me the ability to reach further past my old limitations and pull myself even higher.

Improving your self-image is the greatest single factor I know of for building emotional well-being and happiness. Everybody can have a better self-image. I wish I could perform some magic that would—if only for ten seconds—take away all of the feelings you have that result from past failures and mistakes. If you could rid yourself of all your guilt and regret, you would be one of the happiest people on the face of the earth. You wouldn't have to do anything, you wouldn't have to own anything. Just the fact that you were pleased with who you are would be a wonderful source of satisfaction and happiness.

But have you ever noticed that your attitude about yourself fluctuates? That you seem to have more than one attitude about who and what you are? Aren't there times that you're empowered with feelings of grandeur and a sense of great value, and other times that you feel completely worthless? Sure, we've all had those feelings. That's because, like everything else in the human psyche, your concept of self, your self-image, is multifaceted. In fact, you have three different beliefs about yourself, and they each come from a different place within your mental makeup.

Your Subconscious Self-Image

The first of these three is what I call the *subconscious* self-image. Most psychologists would agree that the major part of your self-image, your real feelings about yourself, dwells in your subconscious. Because these self-concepts are below your conscious awareness, you're not able to examine them directly. Instead, a low self-image manifests itself in *feelings* of inadequacy or lack of value.

The reason many of us don't try to achieve as much as we could is that we secretly feel unworthy to have a better life. In fact, many successful people feel that they don't even deserve what they have. Books have been written about people in high positions, very successful people, who continually worry that someone will discover that they are frauds and that they don't deserve the success they have attained.

Feelings of unworthiness can even rob you of your desires. If you have subconscious misgivings about your ability to accomplish something, or secret feelings of not deserving it, your subconscious may compensate by diminishing your desire for it. You may even decide that you don't want it—without knowing why. The subtle effects of a low subconscious self-image create an inability to overcome fears, a lack of desire to attain goals, and a general feeling of incompetence.

Because our subconscious self-image is traditionally thought of as the sole source of our self-image, I call it the traditional self-image. And there's a good reason the traditional self-image occupies such a prominent place in psychology. As we've already seen, it exerts a tremendous influence on everything you say, think, and do.

Here's how it works. Imagine your subconscious as a room or vault. This is your data storage room. Absolutely everything you've ever heard, seen, thought, or done is in that room. But, because it represents the subconscious, you don't have direct access to it.

So, imagine a door at the front of the room and a guard standing beside it. The guard represents your conscious mind. Now, it would appear that this guard is in charge. After all, if there's a decision to be made, the guard is the one who makes it. But in order to make a decision, he has to have some frame of reference—something to base his decision on. And, although our guard can't go into the room and actually shuffle through the information stored there, he is very definitely affected by what's in there, because he gets a general impression from the total buildup of all this data that he uses to make all of his decisions. But all too often a lot of garbage gets piled up inside the room, and the influence coming from it severely hampers his ability to make a good decision.

How does that garbage get into the room? Well, for most of us, it started with our parents. When we were young, they seemed all-knowing, all-seeing, and all-wise. We accepted everything they said as gospel. But, unfortunately, many of our mothers and fathers didn't understand how much they were affecting our self-image, and so they didn't see the need to make a conscious effort to help build it in a positive way. When parents speak demeaningly to their children, from their Lower Self, out of anger or frustration, those cutting words go straight into that all-important storage room. Then, when the children get old enough to go to school, they quickly find out that their classmates don't know much about encouragement or empowerment either. Everyone knows how cruel children can be. And all of this competitiveness, backbiting, and name-calling go straight into the data storage room.

Now, as if it isn't bad enough that other people throw so much garbage into our room, once we get the hang of it we take over the process ourselves! It's true. People begin teaching us to dislike ourselves when we are very young, and they even show us exactly how it's done so we can keep on demeaning ourselves long after they've gone! We keep repeating what others have taught us how to say: "I've never had any talent in that area"; "I've never been able to do that"; "I'm just not any good at that"; or, "With my luck, the whole thing will come to nothing."

You know, you'd think we would choose to remember the *victories* in our life. The times we inspired people or helped them. But most of us choose to remember our failures and mistakes. So, rather than gaining empowerment from what we've done right, we feel guilty because of all the things we've done wrong. We keep throwing garbage into the room, piling it so high that a smell comes out the door that is horrendous.

Our guard is trying his best to make good decisions, but he can't avoid being influenced by the stench that comes rolling out the door of our data storage room. That's where our feelings of inadequacy come from. And that's one of the main reasons why we have such a hard time building enough desire to overcome our Lower Self.

The traditional self-image is crippling to most of us because our subconscious data room makes for a very effective way for us to continue to live with every mistake we've ever made and every embarrassing moment we've ever experienced. After all, you were always there—you not only saw every rotten thing you've ever done, you even listened in on all those terrible thoughts that no one else even dreamed you were thinking.

But this unconscious feeling you have about yourself is only one of the three ways you evaluate yourself.

Your Sense of Self-Importance

The second concept of self-worth is a function of the conscious mind. It's our sense of self-importance—our ego. It came about because we need to find some way of compensating for the bad feelings that come from our subconscious self-image. Because many of us secretly (and when I say secretly, I mean it's a secret to *us*) harbor feelings of low self-worth, insecurity, and inferiority, we find a way to combat the effects of those feelings and, as a result, our sense of self-importance is born. It's the "self-image" our Lower Self invents in an attempt to find a way to feel better about ourselves.

Of course, we all have weaknesses and insecurities. But putting on a facade that denies them only validates our weakness and adds to our insecurity. That facade is the Lower Self trying to overcome subconscious feelings of inadequacy by seeking self-importance in the world.

These two concepts you hold of yourself—the negative, unconscious feelings that come from the traditional self-image, and the puffed-up attitude of , exaggerated self-importance that arises as a result—are why you can feel like the most wonderful person who ever existed and then, in the next moment, harbor feelings that you're not even worth killing.

Everyone knows someone who is, at heart, the exact opposite of what he forcefully pretends to be. Maybe you know a supermacho guy who has to prove his toughness at every opportunity. If you look closely, you can see that inside he's really a frightened, insecure person who feels constantly threatened. He needs to be treated like a big shot—to prove how important he is, to counteract his lack of self-worth. On the other hand, you may also know someone who doesn't at all mind admitting weaknesses and who is, in fact, a very strong person. People who are secure in their importance act humbly. They have no need to continually prove their worth; they don't have to *act* important because the *are* important.

Now that you have gone to the trouble to learn these two directly opposite concepts of yourself (your traditional self-image and your ego), let me tell you that both are...false. The traditional self-image unfairly beats you over the head with your past mistakes, and your sense of self-importance is just as exaggerated in the other direction.

Your Spiritual Self-Image

Your true self-esteem, your real self-image, lies neither in your consciousness nor in your subconscious. It is at the very center of you...the source of your Higher Self, your spirit. After all, shouldn't the image you hold of yourself reflect who you really are? Your spirit is the source of your conscience, your intuition, and your higher calling. It's where your need for honesty and integrity comes from. It's the source of your motivation to serve others and your inherent, ongoing need for meaning and purpose. This is the real you!

You see, I really believe we are created in the image of our God. Could it be that this part of us is not subject to human frailties and hasn't been a willing participant in all the foolish and selfish things we've done in our lives? Is there a chance that the real us—our spirit—is perfect? Have you ever considered the possibility that the limitations of our physical body (including our brain), and indeed our entire physical existence, are what pulls us toward doing the things we later regret?

In fact, I have chosen to believe that in my true essence—my spiritual identity—I am a perfect being. This is a part of me that only needs to develop and mature.

When I talk about this belief in my seminars, there are always people who ask how we could be perfect if we have not yet developed to our full potential. But just as the acorn is perfect though it hasn't yet become an oak tree, we are complete, we have everything we need to grow to our full stature. Just as the tiny acorn only needs the right conditions of soil, water, and time to grow into a giant tree, we, too, only need the opportunity, the right conditions, and the time to learn, grow, and develop into that which we are destined to be.

So, with all of this in mind, let me give you three things you can do to bolster your self-image.

1. Become Who You Really Are

There are two relatively simple (not easy, but simple) steps to accomplish the shifting of your identity to your inward spiritual being. The first step takes place within that portion of your consciousness you use for formulating your beliefs. Why don't you go in there and *decide* to believe that you're not your physical body? Instead of believing yourself to be your body or

97

even the workings of your mind, why don't you choose to believe that your true identity is buried deep within you? You are, in fact, someone you've never had a chance to experience. You've been so busy paying attention to the churnings of your conscious thoughts and the feelings of your emotions that you have, for your entire life, ignored who and what you really are!

I don't believe it's possible for you to have a better self-image than that of a perfect spiritual being created in the image of your God. You can't get much better than that! The first step, then, in dramatically boosting the value you place on yourself is to choose to believe that you are a spiritual being having a temporary physical experience. Once you've decided to believe that, begin reprogramming your subconscious image of who you are with this positive, healthy, inspiring concept instead of continuing to feed yourself trash.

The second step toward assuming your real identity is the process of turning inward to *experience* the real you. When I first started thinking of myself as a spiritual being, I began wondering how I could get in touch with the real me. That's when I began to discover that our greatest challenge is to turn inward and *discover* the internal self we know so little about.

This was Anwar Sadat's key to finding happiness in his little prison cell. He took the opposite direction from the way most of us seek enjoyment. Since our conscious mind and our five senses point outward to the physical world, most folks seek happiness outside themselves. Sadat, on the other hand, was in that lonely existence, totally cut off from any positive physical environment, and so was forced to turn inward. When he did, he began a journey that ended in the discovery of his real self. What he found was peace, patience, love, and courage—everything he'd always wished he could have.

By experiencing who he really was, he was able to discover another existence, one deep within himself. And it's a richer, more fulfilling existence than any externally based life could ever be.

When people make the mistake of identifying with the Lower Self and live their lives dedicated to the emotional pulls that come from the physical world, they live a shallow existence...on their outer surface.

What does living on the outer surface mean? It means that the person's life consists primarily of participation in the external world. The conscious mind is focused on the five senses, and the five senses relate only to that world. As a result, the person's reality is completely external and physical. Until you learn to stop depending on your five senses for your perception of reality and turn inward—deep within yourself, to find and fully experience your Higher Self—you will continue to live your life in a superficial way, on the outer surface of your being.

Deeper existence brings with it overwhelming benefits. People who have mastered their minds and readjusted their priorities in a way that allows them to experience the inner life have a calmness about them that can't be achieved in any other way.

If you were foolish enough to go out into the ocean during a hurricane, you'd find waves hundreds of feet high. The chaotic power that exists on the surface of the ocean during a major storm is unbelievable. But if you were able to go down a couple of miles beneath the surface, you'd find that the water, even in the middle of the most powerful hurricane, is calm, peaceful, and serene. Likewise, if you live too close to the surface of your being, you're always at the mercy of external forces: Every storm will deal you misery. But beneath that surface is a peaceful, patient, loving, and totally unafraid part of you. This is the *real* you. You only need to find a way to dig inward and get in touch with the source of that inner peace, and then bring it out into your external life.

You can make the same inward journey that enabled Anwar Sadat to make what I believe was the most magnificent discovery of his life. You, too can find your true self-image and discover genuine self-esteem by assuming your real identity.

The only way I've ever found to do this is through the ancient art of meditation. Meditation involves slowing down or even stopping your thoughts. When you learn to shut down the

99

conscious thinking that goes on in your mind, you will automatically drift inward, and, when you do, you'll begin to *discover* who you really are. That's why meditation is such a source of peace and calm for those who practice it. A little later on, I'll give you some instructions on how to start your own daily meditation practice.

2. Get Rid of Old Ghosts

If we are to think better of ourselves, we also need to find a way of ridding ourselves of our "ghosts" from the past—the guilt and regret that keep us from feeling worthy to have what we want.

I could, for instance, allow myself to feel a diminished sense of worth or value because of the life that I led in my younger years. But I refuse to allow past behaviors, no matter how bad they may have been, to diminish who I am today.

Remember, you're attending a *school.* Whatever it was that you may have done in the past isn't nearly as important as what you've become as a result. Nowhere does it say that you have to keep beating yourself up because you had to repeat some lessons in the school of life. Does it really matter that you failed some tests the first time you took them? If you learned from the mistakes and failures in your life and became a better person, little by little, as a result of them, then why not rejoice in the fact you made those mistakes? They contributed to the successful completion of your life's mission. The past is over, never to return. What's important is that you eventually learned those lessons and were able to move on to others. If there's something in your past actions that you really feel bad about, ask yourself one question: Would I do that again today? If the answer is no, then you must have learned from it. You must have grown from it. In the end, it served you and became part of the greater good. That's how we learn, so stop letting it defeat you.

When I look back over my life, I see that a lot of the things I thought were terrible adversities at the time turned out to be an important part of my training. Those situations contributed to

100

who I am, to my maturity and my understanding of life. And I can only assume that it was necessary for me to go through those lessons in order to learn what I needed to learn. Every time I made another blunder there were repercussions. That's the way most of us have to learn. I hadn't learned to look for the lesson in every occurrence yet, so I learned by making a mistake, then suffering the consequences of that mistake, and then saying to myself, "Wow, I don't think I'll do *that* anymore."

The time I spent in the brig in the Navy provided me with powerful reasons and incentives to change. It was one of the bleakest times of my life, yet it was one of the most enlightening and life-changing experiences I've ever had. Do I wish I could have learned that lesson in an easier, nobler way? Of course I do. But do I feel a sense of shame about it? Not on your life. That experience, that mistake, was one of the millions of experiences that have joined together to allow me to become the person I am today.

If you'll show me someone who isn't making mistakes, I'll show you someone who isn't growing. And if I need to make more mistakes in order to grow further, then that's what I'll do. I hope I don't have to; I would rather learn the easy way. But if I do have to embarrass myself and lose my pride, if I have to mess up in order to grow up, then let me start messing up, because growth is what I'm here for.

I tell the folks who attend my prison seminars that I don't care what crime they committed—and I don't. I only care what they are...now. I don't care about what's in the past. And I would suggest you adopt the same philosophy, both for yourself and for others. You must stop giving place to your old ghosts from the past, because if you don't, they will continue to take their toll. And, they can only hold you back...if you choose to let them.

3. *Change Your Outward Self*

The third step in improving your self-image is to start changing how you live your external life.

So far we've restricted our view of increasing self-esteem to inward methods. But it is also very important that you begin demonstrating to yourself outwardly that you truly are becoming the person you want to be. By gaining control of your belief system and understanding the Higher and Lower Self, you can begin to change your behavior and habit patterns in a way that will allow you, step by step, to actually start manifesting more and more of your Higher Self in your thinking and in your actions.

And there's no question, it will take some progress toward changing your outward behavior and circumstances before the task of increasing your self-image can really get underway. It probably won't come as a surprise to you that my self-image got a huge shot in the arm from my financial accomplishments. You know, when I think back on those years when I was so frantically trying to make millions of dollars, I can see the real reason I chose making money as my goal. I was trying to become wealthy because, sub-consciously, I felt it would somehow increase my value or worth. Deep down, I suppose, I was trying to prove to the world that I wasn't inferior; on an even deeper level, I was really trying to prove it to *myself.*

When I did make some progress toward my goal of producing wealth, I *did* feel better about myself. And I found myself with a lot of additional confidence because confidence is a major benefit of an improved self-image.

So I'm certainly not saying outward accomplishments can't improve your opinion of yourself. It's just that I found that outward accomplishment—external performance—won't do it by itself. After I had made all of that money, there was still something severely lacking in my life.

That's why you should also do some work on the purposeful realization of your real identity, and engage your belief system in a way that will allow you to overcome your feelings of guilt or inadequacy.

Then you can begin to produce some physical evidence that you are becoming the person you have chosen to believe yourself to be. At that point, you will want to start using the

102

methods we talked about in Life Lesson 5, and tackle the job of ridding yourself of your old, undesirable habits and replacing them with positive, healthy ones so you can live an external life that you can feel good about.

In this way you can, indeed, become who you want to be. You can renew the dreams you gave up long ago, dreams that seemed too good, or too fantastic, for someone like you. You can be the kind of person to realize those dreams—no matter what they are.

Make the changes, one at a time, beginning with the one you believe will be the easiest. Then, one by one, each successful replacement of another habit will serve as the inspiration for the replacement of the next one. But even while you're still working on the very first one, you'll be able to spend every moment of every day knowing that you are actively *becoming* the person you want to be. Your self-image will get an unbelievable boost, just from that knowledge. You know, none of us will ever be perfect (at least not in this life). But if you know, deep down, that you're getting better every day, that's plenty of reason for you to feel much better about yourself. And that's all it takes to make your life better, richer, and more enjoyable...right now!

PART THREE

Mastering Your Mind
by Managing Your Thoughts

Life Lesson 10

Your Thoughts Make Up Your World

There was a time when I didn't see the need to control what I thought about. I was so busy trying to gain control of my outward actions that I allowed my inner life to just take its own course. Those were the days when I defined the ultimate power as control over my behavior in specific areas in order that I could reach certain goals.

I knew, for instance, that a pleasant, good-natured person who didn't get upset was much more likely to be successful in business than someone who couldn't control his or her emotions and regularly flew off the handle. So I found a way to gain control of my behavior along those lines. And it worked! People loved doing business with me. I was always pleasant, energetic, and enthusiastic...on the outside. I could almost always portray these characteristics, even when inwardly I was seething with rage! I was a fun person for others to be around, but one day it dawned on me that I'd only found a way to give the folks around me a nice environment to enjoy. *My* environment—where *I* lived—was the pits!

I was like one of these people who focus all of their energy on the outside of their house while paying no attention to the inside. Can you imagine someone who works very hard manicuring the lawn, pruning and sculpting all the shrubbery, and keeping the outside of the house clean and freshly painted, but who never lifts a finger to do anything with the inside of his house? Well, that's what I was doing to myself. I had gone to a great deal of effort to fix up my outward behavior so the other people in my life got the benefit of all that pleasantness and encouragement. But you can only stay in a dark, filthy living room and look at other people enjoying your lovely yard for so long; then *you* begin to suffer from the environment you're in.

Of course, this was all happening because, in reality, I wasn't the person I appeared to be. I was only *acting* like that person. In fact, I wasn't even doing a complete job of acting. A good actor submerges himself in his role and *thinks the thoughts* of his character. But I didn't realize the importance of inward participation. To become that person I was pretending to be on the outside, I only had to become a thinker of positive, energetic thoughts. By cleaning up the inside of me, I would have created a totally different, more uplifting, and positive environment for myself.

But I didn't know that, and by thinking negative, spiteful, and critical thoughts, I inadvertently shrouded myself in a negative, bitter environment. Had I only gone about it in the right way, I could have joined those folks that benefited from my enthusiasm. But the people around me were enjoying all the benefits while I was left with the inner knowledge that not only wasn't I an upbeat, enthusiastic person, I was a phony as well!

The Two Lives We Lead

You see, just as you have two selves, you also lead two lives...and you lead them simultaneously. One of them is conducted totally within you. Your internal life is made up of your thoughts, your feelings, and your internal responses to whatever happens to you.

The other life is, interestingly enough, the one we're more familiar with. It's conducted outside ourselves. Our external life is made up of all the things that occur outside us that involve other people and our physical surroundings.

One of these two lives is a lot more important than the other, but unfortunately we have a tendency to emphasize the wrong one. We think that because our external life is conducted out in the open and involves other people, it's the more important one. But we've got it backwards.

For instance, although what you say to other people is certainly important, what you *say* isn't nearly as important as what you *think*. We all know that it's possible to think one thing and say another. In fact, we all do it fairly often. "Oh, I'm so glad to see you" may just be the most often-told lie of this age. Of course, if there can be a noble reason for telling a lie, this one qualifies. Our motivation is kindness. Somehow our society doesn't work very well if we go around speaking truths like, "You know, I'm just not in the mood for you today," and so it's pretty common for us to think one thing and say another. And although we may empower others with what we say, our *thoughts* either empower or discourage *us*. That's because our true personality—negative or positive, happy or sad—results not from our words but from our thoughts. We are much more affected by our internal dialogue than by anything we may say to others.

By the same token, what you do isn't nearly as important as what you *are*. Your beliefs, mindset, attitude, and perception of reality are the inward elements that determine who you are. Your actions may or may not reflect the real you depending on how good an actor you are. You can hide your real self from others but *you* will always know, deep down, who you are...and either suffer or benefit from that inner knowledge.

And when it comes to respect, there's no question that we make the mistake of thinking our biggest need is to gain the respect of others. But, by far, our most important need for respect is our need for *self*-respect.

The Messenger's Box

Imagine, if you will, that I have two good friends who live in separate cities fifty miles apart. The road that connects them runs through a desolate part of the country that's almost uninhabited. It's a barren stretch of road that's seldom traveled.

Now, let's suppose that I decide to go visit both of these friends. I drive to the first city to see my friend Bob. After our visit, I tell Bob that I plan to go to the other city and visit our mutual friend Mary.

At that point he says he'd like to ask a favor. From a drawer he retrieves a little wooden box with a hinged lid, which is

109

closed. He tells me he would like for me to deliver the box to Mary when I drive over to see her. But he says that I'll first have to promise not to look in the box...to deliver it to her unopened. He admits that he has no way to lock the box and there will be nothing to stop me from opening it and peering inside before I get there, but he's depending upon my honor to keep me from doing so.

Well, after I promise that I will under no circumstances look inside, I take the box and begin my journey down the lonely stretch of road to Mary's house.

About halfway there, I look out my windshield and notice that there isn't a living soul as far as I can see. A quick look in my rearview mirror yields the same result behind me. That's when I begin to think, "I could take a look inside that box, and *no one would ever know.*"

Well, there's the dilemma—a Pandora's dilemma, one that would provide a more than adequate moral test for any of us. And the decision I reach will have more dramatic consequences than we might think. If I choose to give in to my Lower Self's curiosity about what's in that box, I make a major announcement to myself about myself. Remember when I told you that we sign up for courses in the school of life by making mistakes? Well, this action is a clear indication that I need an additional class or two in honor. You see, what I'm really saying when I open the box is, "It's all right if *I* know that I'm a sneak, a cheat, and a liar as long as nobody else knows it!"

But that line of thinking is absolutely backwards. You see, when I diminish myself in the eyes of the people who make up my outward life, there's no question that I am adversely effected. But that doesn't take nearly the toll as when I disappoint myself by dropping my standards, because that affects *my* feelings about *me*. In reality, I would be far better off if all of the *rest* of the world—the people who participate in my external life—for some reason thought that I had opened the box...as long as *I* knew I hadn't. You see, then I'd at least be able to maintain the respect of the one person I *must* have respect from: me.

110

Don't Kid Yourself

Our thoughts are more important than any of us imagines. They form our attitude, they add or detract from the quality of our life. Your thoughts, to a large degree, create your external life, but they *are* your internal life.

In his book _As A Man Thinketh_, published in the nineteenth century, James Allen said, "Men imagine that thought can be kept secret, but it cannot; it rapidly crystallizes into habit, and habit solidifies into circumstance." When James Allen talked about thoughts ultimately creating our circumstances he was saying, in effect, that every action originates as a thought. But it goes much further than that.

You see, we fool ourselves into believing that the thoughts that never make it into *physical* activity—the ones that don't become a part of our behavior—aren't important. After all, if we only *thought* about it and didn't act on it, the thought was of no consequence. But our thoughts do not have to result in an external action or behavior for them to have a enormous effect on the quality of our internal life. Don't forget you *live* among all of your thoughts. They make up your world. Your real environment is inside yourself, and what you think about creates the atmosphere in that precious, private place where you reside.

If you want to live a happy, positive, productive life, then you must find a way to keep your thoughts happy, positive, and productive. It's impossible to entertain negative, destructive thoughts and avoid leading a life that matches them. Yes, it is important to say good things, but that isn't good enough. You also have to be *thinking* good things.

If I want to stop worrying, I have to learn how to exclude thoughts that are based on my fears. If I want to stop being resentful, I must stop polluting my inner environment with condemning thoughts and complaints about the people I feel resentment toward. And, as we've just learned, if I want to increase—or even have—self-respect, I must be able to think positive things about myself. And because I can't fool *myself,* the only way I can think those positive thoughts is to actually *be* the person that I display to others. That's why acting doesn't work—it only convinces those people who make up our *outer* life. It isn't enough to look good to them. We must also look good *from the inside.*

Thought Management

If you're going to be able to use your thoughts for your benefit instead of continuing to be held captive by them, you need a way to manage them. An undisciplined, unmanaged mind puts us at the mercy of all of our random, Lower Self thoughts, and deprives us of the power to control our own lives. Most people are enslaved by these kinds of thoughts and keep getting pulled in different directions. Of course that makes it impossible to move consistently toward a worthwhile goal. These people are not only unable to reach a desirable destination, they live in a chaotic atmosphere and are forced to endure an inner life of turmoil that is devoid of any richness or fulfillment.

Using thought management, you can retrain the inner workings of your mind in a way that creates new, positive, and productive habit patterns of thinking. Thought management allows you to decide what you will and won't think about. It allows you to determine *how* you think and what moods will be generated as a result of those thoughts. Thought management is needed in your life in the same way business management is needed in a corporation. Running a business without a management plan results in a chaos that soon bankrupts the operation. And whether you've ever realized it or not, you need to manage your thoughts—just as you would an important business operation—by developing a plan to accomplish your mental goals and then finding a way to make that plan a reality.

I won't try to kid you. It isn't easy. But over a period of time your thought management efforts can totally retrain your subconscious in a way that will develop good thought management habits. Remember, your thinking is *habitual,* just like most of the other things you do. You can create a fresher, more positive mental environment by developing a new set of habitual thought patterns that will allow you a deeper, richer life. And, in the bargain, you'll find the self-control necessary to do virtually anything you want to do with your external life.

Back when I first decided to become a real estate salesman, I worked for a broker named Jack Winton. Jack now lives in El Paso, Texas, and we have remained good friends throughout the years. As long as I've known him, he's possessed a rather unique talent. Jack has always taken charge of creating his own mental environment. The rest of us around the office always allowed our external circumstances to determine our moods. But Jack didn't. He was always in a positive, jovial frame of mind—and it wasn't just an act. It became obvious to me early on that he had purposely taken control of his thoughts. As a result, he always required himself to think in a happy, encouraging way. It didn't seem to matter much to him if things were going well, or if they weren't. He seemed almost as happy when a deal fell through as when a big contract had just been written. It didn't make any difference if it was a dreary, miserable day or a wonderful sunny one. Jack met them all the same way—he was happy and full of life. I remember thinking back then how unusual it was that he didn't seem to depend on his outward circumstances for his happiness. And, boy, did I envy him for it.

Then, over the years, I ran into a couple of techniques that now make up the cornerstone of my thought management efforts. The first I call "*thought replacement*" or "throwing away a thought," and the other, "*planned response.*" Both of these methods require some effort and practice, but take it from me: The benefits you can receive from them will be well worth your time.

Thought Replacement

This is a simple way to replace your undesirable thoughts with ones that are more positive and uplifting. The first thing you're going to do is to identify the thoughts you have that are counterproductive; they're the ones you want to remove from your inner life. They could be feelings of bitterness, fear, or just

113

the negative "judging" of your circumstances or of other people. No one is better qualified than you to find and target the thoughts that bring you down and make your life less enjoyable and satisfying.

As we've already learned, it's almost impossible to keep a thought from coming into your mind. But that doesn't mean that you have to *dwell* on it. When you give in to those thoughts and devote time to entertaining them, they make a contribution to your attitude. Then you find yourself harboring, without knowing why, a mind-set that's negative and counterproductive. But an undesirable thought that you're able to immediately reject—one that you refuse to ponder and consider—never has a chance to take hold and tear down your inner peace.

Once you've decided on the thoughts you *don't* want to think about, you need to come up with better thoughts to replace them. You can't just decide to throw a thought out; you must instead *replace* it with a different thought. And you can't afford to wait until the unwanted thought presents itself before you decide on its replacement. If you do, you'll have the same problem that befell the little boy who was told not to think of a pink elephant. Remember, the way to avoid thinking about something is to think about something else. Let me give you an example.

If you're dealing with self-doubt or feelings of inadequacy, think back and remember a situation in which you were truly magnificent and triumphant. Then pick one of your proudest moments, a time when you handled things beautifully, when people admired your actions and told you so. Remember every detail of the incident and put a vivid picture of it in your mind. It will then be standing by, ready to use.

Now, anytime those old feelings of doubt and inadequacy arise, you can get rid of them by replacing them with the vivid picture of the triumphant moment you have standing by. As soon as you do, the old thought or feeling will leave. It has to— you can't keep them both in your mind at the same time. It's high time we found a way to take advantage of the fact that we can't think two thoughts at once. After all, we really do have a choice as to the kinds of thoughts we allow to occupy that precious conscious chamber, and whatever we fill it with will automatically exclude everything else.

We already know how to exclude thoughts. The mistake we all make is excluding the *good* ones and inadvertently allowing our nonproductive, fearful, and destructive thoughts to dominate our inner life, and control our outer one as well.

Planned Response

Planned Response is very similar to thought replacement, but there is a difference. While thought replacement is learning to *think* in more positive ways, planned response is a means of changing how you *react* to situations and circumstances in your life. Impatience is a response to things not moving as fast as they could. Outbursts of anger and criticism are responses to something that happened that you didn't agree with. You see, we've trained ourselves to react or respond to some situations in certain ways—ways we often later regret.

Thought replacement takes place completely within our inward environment—our thinking—but planned response deals also with outward behavior. This means that in addition to recognizing the thoughts that bring on the undesired reaction, we must also replace the reaction itself.

Let's use anger as an example. When someone does something that "makes you mad," like most of us you probably respond in a knee-jerk manner by simply allowing your habitual emotional patterns to play out as they have thousands of times before. And when it's over and your better judgment again takes charge, you find yourself having to apologize for your actions and wishing you could have stayed in control.

After all, being angry, judgmental, and constantly critical of other people is self-destructive behavior. You cannot harbor these kinds of thoughts without severely wounding your ability to love yourself. Grouchy, spiteful complainers can't be happy. It's impossible. I've never met a happy hater.

As in thought replacement, in planned response the first two steps are to identify the unwanted thoughts and attitudes that make up the response you want to change, and then to decide on a more appropriate reaction that you can substitute for them when the need arises.

The freeway at rush hour can provide us with a wonderful opportunity to see how this might work. I must admit that I've done more than a little steering wheel pounding myself. How many times have you arrived at work having ruined a perfectly good day by boiling over inside because of something another driver did on the highway?

Of course the ridiculous part of this whole thing is that the person who caused you all that mental turmoil has no idea what he did and couldn't care less. He probably showed up at work in a wonderful mood and thoroughly enjoyed the rest of the day!

Well, let's figure out an alternative response. We need to decide now, before we even get in the car—while we're in a calm, objective, rational frame of mind—how we're going to react the next time this happens. What if we decided that instead of allowing ourselves to get upset by entertaining all that inner dialogue about "how can people be so stupid" and "they ought to take away his driver's license," we simply choose to reflect on a little piece of logic? When it happens the next time, you might remind yourself that the person in the other car didn't mean to cause you any grief. He's just not a very good driver, and it's pretty foolish to get all upset over a total stranger's incompetence! And, of course, because our thoughts generate our behavior, our new attitude will automatically cause (or at least allow) us to act in a totally different way. So cap all this off by giving the other driver a friendly wave and silently wish him well as he goes on his way. Now you can both feel good about your day.

Once you start using planned response, it's important to fight *every* battle. E*very* time the old response rears its head, you must make the attempt to change your behavior. You see, the more times you attempt the replacement—the longer you stay with the program—the more you will convince your subconscious that you mean business. Persistence and consistency are the keys to making it work for you.

116

Of course it's unrealistic to expect to win all of these battles at the beginning. Total victory is your ultimate goal, but initially you'll more than likely find that you can only win the small ones. But these little victories are very important. They give you some continuing evidence that the plan is working and they contribute to the retraining process. When your subconscious is retrained, even a little, by winning a small battle, progress has been made. Obviously, at the beginning, your emotional reaction in a lot of these episodes will overpower your planned response. But if you keep trying, the battles you do win will become larger and more significant, until eventually nothing outside of you will be able to take control of your feelings and make you endure the negativity that spoils your inward atmosphere.

Remember, the most important thing you'll ever do is the work you conduct *inside yourself.* The biggest struggles you have in life will be the inner ones, and the victories you win in these struggles will, in the final result, mean more to you than anything else you do. You will either gain control of your thoughts...or they will remain in control of you. And it's all a matter of what you choose to think about.

Life Lesson 11

You Have to Turn Inward
Before You Can Discover the Real You

A couple of years ago, I was putting a new seminar together in Tampa, Florida. Actually, I was developing it and teaching it simultaneously because a long time ago I found out that some of my best ideas occur to me when I'm in front of a group.

It was going very well, until I hit one particular section that I just couldn't get right. I knew each individual part of the concept, but I couldn't figure out how to put them all together so they'd make sense. I couldn't see the big picture, and so during the three days I worked on that section, I didn't get any further than where I was when I started.

I was down to the wire. It was late in the afternoon and I was running out of time to print up the material for that evening's meeting. I was under a lot of pressure: These folks were going to show up and I didn't have anything to tell them.

So, I did the most illogical thing I could have done. With a legal pad and a pen in hand, I walked out to the pool, lay down in a chaise lounge, closed my eyes, and refused to think.

First I calmed myself, and all the pressure went away. Then I began to feel peaceful. At that point I was feeling good, and my conscious mind started to entreat, "I can figure it out now, I can figure it out now." But I had promised myself 30 minutes without thinking, so I refused to entertain those thoughts. (I learned this technique when I first began meditating a number of years ago.) Once I reached a state of stillness and began to feel a familiar, quiet calm, then and only then did I allow myself to do some deeper thinking—which is what I call the "thinking" I do while meditating. It's not really thinking at all, it's more like being still and waiting for answers. I continued this way for a while in my calm, meditative state.

119

Then the most incredible thing happened. Ideas began to flow into my conscious mind almost in packaged form—it was as if they all showed up at once instead of coming one by one as they usually do. I grabbed the pen and pad and began to write feverishly, as if taking dictation from someone speaking faster than I could write. It took ten minutes to write it all down. After being totally frustrated for three days, I had what I needed after only forty-five minutes—ten minutes to write it, and the other thirty-five to get into a state of mind that would allow me to access the capability to create it.

Some people say that this is merely the tapping of the resources of your subconscious mind, which, of course, is indeed much more powerful and knowledgeable than your conscious mind. After all, it has stored everything you've ever learned, and it's very educated and wise. It certainly seems reasonable that tapping the subconscious would give us access to answers we ordinarily couldn't come up with.

But others say the ability to find answers is escalated because meditation taps directly into your all-knowing spirit. You know, almost every religion believes that God dwells within us. And if you have an all-knowing higher power dwelling in or with your spirit, then you have, in your spirit, access to all the knowledge in the universe. If this is the case, then we would be smart to re-direct a major portion of our efforts to seek knowledge toward discovering our inner self. In fact, now that I've spent some time meditating, I'm amazed that we insist upon continuing to look outside ourselves for answers that are obviously not there. If the creator of the universe, who obviously possesses all the knowledge and wisdom that there is, resides in or with my spirit, then my spirit has access to every conceivable answer. Is it possible that a part of you already knows everything and it's just that we haven't been able to get in touch with that part of ourselves that keeps us from having all the wisdom we could ever want? That possibility is one of the many reasons that turning inward, through meditation, and getting in touch with the real you is so important.

How It All Began

I began using meditation almost by accident. It was one of those things I just stumbled onto.

It started when I realized how important it was to have control over my thoughts. I began looking for techniques and methods that would allow me to gain better control over what goes on in my mind. I read every book I could find on mind control and mental self-mastery, and although very few of them talked about meditation directly, it seemed that most of them made some mention of it in one way or another. It was from reading these side discussions that I came to understand that meditation is the practice of focusing of all of your concentration on one thing to the exclusion of all other thoughts.

The idea began to develop that I could strengthen and discipline my mind by using meditation as a mental exercise in the same way that we use physical exercise to strengthen the muscles of the body. The more I thought about the idea, the better I liked it. Oh, it seemed pretty far out for a west Texas country boy—somehow I just couldn't visualize myself sitting in the middle of the floor with my legs in a knot, holding my hands up in the air with my thumbs and index fingers together—but I have to admit it was intriguing. I reflected on the fact that meditation has been practiced for thousands of years, because I've learned that if something stays around for very long, there is usually some validity to it. And besides, I knew if I was going to gain control of the workings of my conscious mind to the point that I could decide what I would think about, I was going to have to do something radically different than I'd ever done before. And meditation was certainly that.

So, I went down to a local bookstore and picked up a copy of the only book they had on the subject. It was _How to Meditate_ by Lawrence LeShan, and it's a book I still highly recommend. LeShan is far from being some kind of New Age guru. He's a psychologist who approaches meditation from a logical, down-to-earth, Western standpoint—one that I could easily relate to.

Of course, he also had a lot of things to say about meditation that I wasn't ready for or interested in. As far as I was concerned, the spiritual aspects of the practice belonged to other religions, and I was leery of them because I was afraid of straying too far from my own religious beliefs.

The book did, however, provide me with plenty of information about what I *was* looking for—the disciplining and training of my conscious mind. Meditation in its practice is a very simple concept. It is a method of stilling the conscious mind. I suppose that it's impossible to make your mind totally blank (my friend, Ed Foreman, says, "If you did... how would you know?"). So the idea is not to stop thinking completely as much as it is to still or slow the workings of your mind by focusing your attention on some mundane concept or object so intently that you do not allow your mind to "wander."

By the time I had read enough to know what meditation was all about, I reasoned that if I could spend some time focusing my mind in a way that kept random thoughts from entering it, I would be training myself in the skill necessary to master my mind.

Well, it turns out that there are literally thousands of techniques in meditation and probably thousands of ways to practice each one of them. After the book gave me an overview of the various methods, I picked one and decided to give it a try.

My First Meditation

I had decided to use a method that consisted of counting breaths. We all know how important breathing is to the physical body, but apparently there's always been a feeling that the breath is special to the human spirit too. For centuries, it seems, paying attention to and counting breaths has been a staple in meditative techniques.

Following the instructions, I sat down in a comfortable chair, leaned back, closed my eyes, and completely relaxed. After a brief period of focusing on my body, purposely relaxing each group of muscles, I turned my attention to my breathing. I started counting my breaths from one to four, over and over again. Soon I realized that it was helpful to add the word "and" each time I inhaled so I would have something to keep me mentally involved the entire time. As I exhaled, I would say—not aloud but in my mind— the word "one." Then, as I inhaled, I would say "and," then, exhaling, "two," inhaling, "and...three...and...four"...and so on.

Yes, it's really that simple...and that terribly difficult. The problem, of course, is the stream of thoughts that keep rushing, uninvited, into your mind. The first four or five times through the sequence I was pretty well able to restrict my concentration to the counting, because the process was new and interesting to me. But it wasn't long before two things began to happen. First, without realizing it, I was teaching my subconscious how to count my breaths. As always, it was the silent observer watching me do something, learning the procedure so it could be ready to take over as it does so much of the time.

The second thing was that, as my boredom level increased, my attention began to wander. A thought would pop into my mind, totally unannounced. It might have to do with a problem I'd been trying to solve or maybe something as simple as what I'd like to have for lunch that day. But all of those renegade thoughts, no matter what they were about, had the same effect...they captured my attention. I'd be rolling right along, "one...and...two...and," then here would come a thought. "I forgot to call Fred! I hope he isn't upset...." And, at that point, the phone call to Fred was all I was thinking about. Then, all of a sudden, it would dawn on me that I was supposed to be counting my breaths! Now, when I checked on the status of my meditation, sure enough I *am* counting breaths—except that it's not me counting, it's my subconscious. You see, I've already begun to form a habit...a habit that frees up my conscious mind from having to meditate so I can think about something else! (I knew it was my subconscious doing the counting because I was saying "and...eight...and...nine...." My subconscious hadn't quite mastered the fine point of stopping at "four" and returning to "one" each time!)

123

So I would refocus my attention and begin counting again. This happened to me literally hundreds of times. It was like taking a totally undisciplined little puppy out for a walk on a leash. I know where I want him to go—straight down the sidewalk—and he probably does too. But that isn't his agenda. His motivation is curiosity. And so every time we take off in the right direction, something attracts his attention and he runs over and begins to sniff whatever it is. Of course, once I realize that he's gone astray, I pull on his leash and bring him back on the right path and we then start the whole process again.

My mind acted just like that little puppy. A thought that was completely unrelated to my meditation would go skipping through my mind, singing its own little song, and, sure enough, I would take the bait. When I began entertaining that thought—allowing it to unfold and bring forth all of its related thoughts—it would take me captive! There isn't any other way to say it. I was continually trying to restrict my attention to the counting of my breaths, but, one after another, those thoughts would come along and make me forget what I was doing. Then, just as with the puppy on the leash, I would have to pull my attention back to the discipline and begin again.

Well, if I hadn't read so many wonderful things about what meditation could do for me, I would have given up after the first fifteen minutes. It's that hard, it's that discouraging, and it's that boring. (Hey, if it was easy, everyone would be doing it.) Fortunately, however, LeShan's book had warned me about the early pitfalls and had assured me that things would get much better if I would just stay with it. And he was right. A lot of people have come to me after a short period of trying to meditate and told me that they just weren't capable of stilling their minds. I always have to laugh when I hear that—partly because I can genuinely relate to what they're saying, but mainly because I now realize that someone new to meditation who is frustrated about his progress is like someone who's been taking guitar lessons for a week complaining that he can't play "Malaguena." It takes a lot of practice to become proficient at meditating. And as I practiced, it got much easier, and even pleasurable.

As I had hoped, meditation turned out to be a perfect mental exercise for strengthening and disciplining my mind. My mind became more focused and organized, and it wasn't long before I enjoyed a new clarity and an increased ability to concentrate.

But, to my surprise, I also began benefiting in ways I hadn't dreamed of. The increase in mental strength I got from meditation was only one of many life-changing benefits.

A Deeper, Richer Existence

Meditation is not only a mystery to us Westerners, it's also a practice that's received a lot of bad press and, as a result, is really misunderstood. We Americans are very reluctant to borrow customs and practices from other parts of the world, especially if they have to do with spiritual matters. Most folks think meditation is strictly a religious practice that can't be used outside of the spiritual activities of the Far Eastern religions. But being afraid to meditate because people of other religions use it in their spiritual practices is like refusing to kneel because people of other religions do so when they pray.

When I first started using meditation, I saw it strictly as a secular mental exercise. My plan was to keep it completely separate from my religious views and practices. I only partially upheld this goal, though.

You see, while meditation doesn't have to be a religious activity, it is, very definitely, a *spiritual* one. Do you remember earlier when I talked about turning inward and getting in touch with the spiritual you? Well, meditation helps you access that spiritual you.

The only way you'll ever sink deep enough within yourself to experience your spiritual identity is to slip in *between your thoughts.* You see, most of us have so much mental chaos going on that our thoughts are jammed together in our minds, and they run along, one following immediately on the heels of another. Because they never stop, they don't allow us to be aware of anything except this endless stream of intellectual activity. If you can find a way to stop those thoughts for just a fraction of a

125

second, you will then slip in between them. And when you slip between your thoughts and stop paying attention to who you believe you are, you have the opportunity to find out who you really are.

Each of us, at the very center of our being, is incredibly peaceful, unbelievably loving, and patient beyond measure. You can find out what perfection feels like if you can just go deep enough to find it within yourself.

And you'll also discover the immense source of knowledge deep within you. You may look for profound answers about life in the material world, but they are simply not there. They're inside—in the vast galaxy of your inner consciousness. And stilling your conscious mind, shutting off your five senses, and turning inward is the first step toward reaching this inner storehouse of knowledge.

When you do this, you automatically drift downward toward an awareness of a much deeper, richer existence. That's what's spiritual about meditation. No matter what your religious beliefs are, when you pray, you're much more likely to hear the answer if you're in touch with your spirit. If your spiritual identity goes unnoticed because you're totally preoccupied with the boombox blaring of all those conscious thoughts, how can you have any spiritual awareness? How can you hear the small, still voice that we all hope will help guide us through this life? Meditation provides a way to develop your spiritual awareness.

But, unfortunately, that's far from the reputation it has received in this part of the world. I've even heard it said that meditation was a tool of the devil—that when you suspend your conscious thoughts it gives the devil access to your mind, and he would then take you over and, I suppose, make you into some kind of evil person. Well, all I can say is that I've been meditating a long time and nothing like that has ever happened to me.

If, however, you can't shake the idea that meditation is somehow contrary to your concept of religion, let me remind you that you can meditate by focusing your concentration on anything, including scriptures, religious sayings, or even

126

prayers. A lot of Christians, for instance, meditate on the Lord's Prayer, or portions of the Sermon on the Mount. Now I ask you, how could you possibly be inviting some evil power into yourself by quieting your mind and not allowing yourself to think about anything but a part of the teachings of your chosen religion?

Meditation can be used by anyone, and it can be used for a variety of purposes. The basic effect, however, seems to be the same for everyone who tries it. It's been described by many people as a feeling of "coming home." And every meditator agrees that it allows you to settle into a calmness that somehow just feels like a more real you.

Closing Out the Storm

We all see the benefit of taking a yearly vacation to get away from our day-to-day physical surroundings. But how would you like to take a "vacation" from the turmoil of your conscious mind? Well, you can. That's one of the many benefits of meditation.

Once you get proficient at the practice of meditation, you enter into an altered state of consciousness. Some call it "superconsciousness," but I like to refer to it as "the alpha state." The alpha state gets its name from the slower, alpha brain waves—measurable on an EEG—that normally come from a person who is in the "twilight" area of consciousness that each of us experiences just before going to sleep at night and on first awakening each morning.

Once you've been in the alpha (meditative) state for a few minutes, a wonderful calmness begins to pervade your entire being. And, when you've completely mastered putting yourself deeply into that state, you'll discover an incredible inner peace— a feeling unlike anything you've ever experienced. I believe this state of calmness and peace is a result of moving into and experiencing your spiritual self.

A few minutes of meditation is the very best stress reliever I've ever discovered. It allows you the opportunity to take a vacation from everything...including *yourself.* I read a book some time ago by a fellow meditator. (Unfortunately, I've misplaced the book and I can't remember the title or the author's name.) He relayed a story that provides a great way to understand the calming effect of meditation. His office had windows that were apparently much like shutters. One day he left them unlocked, and while he was out, an unexpected storm came up, with bitterly cold wind. When he returned to his office, the storm was still going strong, and he found that the windows had been blown open and papers were scattered all over the office. When he went in, the room was frigid, and the wind was still blowing all those papers around and banging the windows back and forth.

The first thing he did was close the windows to keep the storm outside. He then started a fire in the fireplace and picked up all of his papers, putting them all in order and neatly stacking them where they belonged. A few minutes later, the fire was crackling, and he was all toasty and comfortable in his newly restored office, protected against the storm raging outside.

He said that the experience couldn't help reminding him that our five senses are our windows to the world. And if we don't have some means, every now and then, to close those windows during external storms, we'll be at their mercy each time they come around. Meditation provides an escape of total peace. After all, if you could stop thinking, you wouldn't be aware of *any* of your problems or the stress you experience as a result of them! For that brief period of time each day, you can literally forget all your cares and be suspended in a wonderfully secure and peaceful place deep within yourself. Without anything to weigh it down, your mind has a chance to refresh and rejuvenate itself. (If you are interested in learning more about meditation, see page 177.)

As strange as it sounds, everything that's really worthwhile in this life is inside you, not outside. If you ever have a chance to choose between all the riches the world has to offer and inner peace, don't even give it a second thought. Inner peace is by far the better bargain. Calmness, serenity, and clarity of mind must be the first steps in any search for happiness. And you simply can't find any of those things outside yourself. A life devoted entirely to the outward physical realm and the pursuit of material possessions will always leave something lacking. When we lead a strictly outward life, we ignore and try to deny our true identity. But let's face it; there just isn't any peace in not knowing who you are. The harder we run toward the promises of our outward desires, the further we'll distance ourselves from everything we secretly desire. It's only when we turn inward by shutting off the rest of the world and stopping our random, chaotic thoughts that we can discover what life is really all about. It's about human dignity, caring, compassion, and a genuine sense of belonging. And those things are available to you...but they're only available within.

Life Lesson 12

There's Only One Time and One Place
You Can Be Happy

Have you ever noticed that everybody seems to be waiting on something to happen before they can be happy? There's a terrible old joke that I love—in fact, I never miss a chance to tell it...including this one. It's about a very old couple. He was ninety eight, she was ninety six, and they'd been married for seventy five years when they showed up in divorce court. The judge, realizing that they had been married longer than he'd been alive, couldn't resist asking the obvious. If these old folks were as incompatible as they claimed to be, why had they waited so long to get a divorce? The old man didn't hesitate. He looked the judge in the eye and said, "We were waiting for the kids to die."

We're all waiting on something to make us happy. It starts as early as grade school. We all remember what we thought would make us happy when we were in grade school—junior high! After all, those kids were using pens instead of pencils and anybody could see that they were really cool. We just knew that as soon as we got to junior high we'd be so happy.

But, unfortunately, by the time we got to junior high, happiness had moved on to high school. I mean, after all, those kids are playing football and dating, while we have to be in bed by *ten!* Yeah, we'll really be happy just as soon as we get to high school.

But when we got our chance at high school, somebody's brother has gone off to college and he's loving it. The rumor is that college professors don't even care whether you come to class or not! Now *that's* happiness!

Now, it isn't long after we finally get to college that we meet that certain special someone and fall in love. Under the stars we spend hours together saying things like, "If we can just get the drudgery of this school work out of the way and get our diplomas, we can buy a home of our own and *start our little family*, and oh, we'll be so happy then!"

Of course, when we do have a couple of kids, who end up yelling and screaming all through the house, we turn to each other with knowing looks on our faces and say through clenched teeth, "If we can just get these kids raised and out of here...we'll be so happy and relaxed then."

What we have here is a perpetual version of the grass is greener on the other side. We're not really waiting on something to happen so we can be happy, we're just making excuses for the fact that we don't know *how to be* happy. Living your life waiting on some event that is supposed to somehow magically transform you into a happy person is nothing more than another *habit* —a way of living life that avoids having to face the truth, which is that we're not happy because we don't know enough *about* happiness to make it a reality in our lives.

You see, there's only one time and one place you can be happy. That one time is right now and that one place is right here. And that's because right here and right now is all there ever is. Your life—no matter how many years it lasts—will always be made up of *this moment.* Life is an endless series of...right nows. Everybody knows that yesterday is gone and will never be back, so any missed chance at yesterday's happiness is lost forever. But what most of us don't realize is that tomorrow never comes. Today is not followed by tomorrow; today is *always* followed by...*another today.* When is the last time you asked someone what day it was and, after a quick glance at the calendar, the person responded, "It's tomorrow!" No, that never happens. It will always be right now.

A major key to attaining happiness is the ability to savor and appreciate this moment—no matter what your outward circumstances might be—because this moment is the only time you'll ever have available to you to be happy.

When we reflect on this obvious truth, we all think we already know it. But, in fact, most of us don't. I know I didn't...not for a long, long time. I was continually seduced by

132

the things other people seemed to be enjoying. Did you ever notice that life *looks* like so much more fun on other people than it feels like on *you?* I used to see people having a good time at some recreational activity and think because they were having so much fun at it, I could too. There was a time or two that I remember driving past a golf course and seeing those country club types playing golf and having a wonderful time. They'd be out there with those cute little hats and their golf shirts and, of course, those fancy shoes with the spikes sticking out the bottom of them. Then one of them would hit the ball, obviously enjoying every moment, and I'd say, "Boy, that looks fun. I think I'll take up golf." So, I'd go down and get me one of those little hats along with the shirt, the shoes, and a set of clubs, but you know something, when I got out on the course with all that stuff, I'd find out that there was nothing special about being out there. It was just me...playing golf. I wasn't having nearly as much fun as those folks seemed to be having when I watched them doing the very same thing. You see, my real problem was that I didn't have the ability to savor and enjoy the moment...no matter how much fun what I was doing was supposed to be.

If you're not happy wherever you are, in the middle of whatever your circumstances happen to be, then your problem is not that the right circumstances haven't come along; your problem is that you don't know *how* to be happy.

Be Here Now

A few years ago, Ram Dass, the Harvard professor turned New Age guru, coined a phrase and titled one of his first books with it. *Be Here Now* was his solution to our tendency to put off happiness. Now, I realize that, when you first consider them, those three words seem ridiculously simple. But they make a very important point that most of us have not bothered to think about or taken the time to understand. Let me see if I can't give you an idea how truly profound this little phrase is.

When I was in my twenties and early thirties, I had the habit of driving way too fast. And my early driving record was loaded with speeding tickets to prove it. But it wasn't until just a few years ago that I understood *why* I always had to drive so fast. It was because I wasn't in the car! Oh, my body was in the car all right, but my mind was already at my destination. I spent all of my time thinking about where I was going, mentally putting myself there. I suppose it was in an effort to tell myself what a good time I would have when I got there. And of course, because my mind wasn't in the car, it was impossible for me to enjoy the journey. I didn't know anything about "savoring the moment" because I hadn't gotten far enough in the school of life to learn that life is as much about taking the trip as it is about arriving at the destination. I couldn't enjoy the beautiful scenery along the way or the comfort and safety of the inside of my car.

So the obvious solution for me was to drive fast...to have my body catch up with my mind so I could enjoy my life. But, alas, by the time I managed to get my body to that destination, my mind had moved on to the next one. You see, I really mean it when I say that not staying in the present moment is a habit. It was certainly my habit. There wasn't any way I was ever going to enjoy *any* of my life because I wasn't there at the time! Ram Dass would have said that I simply didn't have the ability to be here now, and he sure would have been right.

A year or so after my divorce, I decided I would take one of those "quality" trips with my fifteen-year-old daughter, Michelle. I really knocked myself out. I rented a motor home and stocked it with everything we'd need for a weeklong, superfun vacation. Then we got in and drove that thing all the way to Yellowstone National Park.

Boy, was that trip a disaster! Oh, it was a good idea, but we just didn't have the ability to pull it off. It ended up being among the most miserable weeks either of us has ever spent anytime, anywhere. And there was one simple reason it all went wrong. Neither of us were there. The motor home ended up in Yellowstone National Park, and so did our bodies. But Michelle was back at home with her boyfriend—she thought about him every moment—and I was mentally back at the office doing business. Because our minds were elsewhere, we missed out on

134

the magnificence of Yellowstone. We could have drunk in the beauty and the splendor of that awesome wonder of nature, but we didn't. And most of all, a father and daughter who truly loved each other missed an opportunity to spend some quality time together because they didn't have the ability to bring their minds together with their bodies for the purpose of enjoying what's happening...right now.

Have you ever noticed that there are people who seem to thoroughly enjoy just *breathing*? Enjoyment of the present moment is a wonderful skill that can enable you to lead a happy, productive, fulfilling life—not just when something exciting or unusual is happening, but all the time, every moment of every day. And make no mistake, those people are not happy because there's something different or unusual about them. They have simply acquired an ability that makes *all* of their life special and meaningful. They're operating by their own definition of happiness.

How Do You Define Happiness?

Take a quick look below:

Unhappiness ├──────────────────────┤ Happiness

This chart represents the full spectrum of enjoyment, ranging all the way from "unhappiness" to "happiness." The short vertical line to the left represents unhappiness. This is when someone hits you over the head with a hammer. This is when your spouse asks for a divorce, or the day you get fired. These are the things that would cause *anyone* to be unhappy.

But look at the vertical line to the right. It represents happiness. And I don't mean just everyday, average happiness, I mean ecstatic, joyful, busting-at-the-seams happiness. This is when you win the lottery or get a big, unexpected promotion. It's your wedding day, and all of the other very special, unusual times that are sprinkled throughout your life. These are the

135

times that make everyone happy...whether they know anything about happiness or not.

Now, I have a question for you. Do you see the long span of horizontal line between the two vertical marks? What is that? If everything to the left of the horizontal line represents sadness and everything to the right of it indicates extreme bliss, then what is all of that area in between? Well, I'll tell you what it is. It's most of your life! And what is that going to be to you?

You see, as with everything else in life, the first thing you have to do before you achieve something is define it. In almost everything you try to accomplish in life, whether you win or lose depends on how you define the victory. In this case, the victory is happiness. And if you limit your definition of happiness to those exciting, special moments we all get a chance to enjoy from time to time, the vast majority of your life will seem dull, lackluster and, as a result, unhappy.

Luckily it dawned on me one day that there are two basic ways to arrive at your definition of happiness. (Be careful now, because the definition you pick will determine how much happiness will be available for you to enjoy.)   You can approach it directly by defining happiness as the *absence of unhappiness*, or you can go at it from the opposite direction by concluding that unhappiness is the *absence of happiness*. Both definitions create an idea of what happiness is, but can you see the enormous difference between the two?   A lot of people simply refuse to be happy unless something really wonderful is happening to *make* them happy.   But if you decide that happiness is the absence of unhappiness, you are then perfectly free to enjoy each and every moment of your life as long as some tragedy isn't preventing you from enjoying it. I've learned not to expect my circumstances to make me happy. It is *my* responsibility to be happy, as long as my circumstances don't prevent it.

If you adopt the first definition, the vast majority of that horizontal line—the line that makes up most of your life—is happiness.

The biggest mistake most of us make in looking for happiness is that we look for the wrong things. What we ought to be seeking is *opportunity*—the opportunity to find happiness within ourselves. But, instead, we depend on external stimulus. We look for exciting, entertaining outward activities. But all those activities—the TV, the movies, the meals, the sex—are not your life. They are, instead, the *distractions that keep you from finding your life.*

Getting to Know Yourself

As soon as I began to see all of this, I started looking for a way to train myself to be here now. I started by doing something that I really didn't like to do. I began spending some time...alone. You see, the first thing we have to do in order to settle into the moment is to allow our selves some time without the distractions we've always used for enjoying life.

So, purposely spend some time by yourself. It might be in a favorite room, or it might be outside in some secluded spot. Once you're alone, make it a point to get quiet and still. And then, here's the real key to being here now...only entertain the thoughts that have to do with what's happening in the present moment. Don't allow yourself to think about anything that isn't happening *now*. You see, as you train yourself to restrict your thoughts to the moment, you'll be teaching yourself the art of being here now.

Now I know what you're thinking. You're saying, "If I'm all alone, sitting quiet and still, not doing anything, how can I possibly restrict my thoughts to the nothingness of that moment?" But that's just the point. There is a lot going on at that place and time in your life that you've trained yourself not to notice. Your reality simply doesn't include the thousands of tiny occurrences you've taught yourself to ignore.

Well, it's time to relearn what life is really all about. Slow everything down. Take the time to notice all of the things that happen around you that you're normally not aware of. Notice the temperature. Pay some attention to your breathing. Take the

137

time to study a blade of grass or a leaf and really think about what you're looking at. Spend some time looking at your hand. You know, scientists have filled up rooms full of computers trying to emulate the human hand, but they haven't even come close. You *own* one! Look at it—spend some time in awe of it.

The trick is to learn how to disconnect from all of the thoughts of the dead past and the imagined future. After all, neither of them is a part of your present reality. The past will never return and the future isn't here yet. The only thing we can be sure of is what's happening now, and it's this moment we must get thoroughly acquainted with so we can learn to enjoy and appreciate it. Being here now will give you the ability to savor what Joseph Campbell called the "rapture of living." I don't think he ever wrote about the rapture of watching television or going to movies or having a seven-course meal or even riding a roller coaster. No, you need to find out enough about your life to be able to see each moment of it as a precious treasure to be savored and enjoyed.

Not long ago, I met a man who had sold his business and retired and then a short time later was diagnosed with terminal cancer. As soon as he began telling me that, I started to offer my condolences. But he stopped me midsentence and said, "Oh, no, don't feel sorry for me, Joe...you see, in a very real way, cancer is the best thing that ever happened to me." Well, I was dumbfounded by that statement and I shut my mouth and listened intently as he went on to tell me how his life had taken on a great deal more meaning since he learned that he was soon going to lose it. He said he didn't know how much time he had left, but no matter how short the rest of his life might be, it would mean more to him than all of the time he'd had up until then. He told me that he now appreciates and savors every breath he takes. He talked about the fact that he never lets a day go by without telling everyone in his family that he loves them. And then he said, "As strange as it might sound, I really am thankful to the cancer. It taught me how to live life, and I wouldn't trade a day of what I have now for a year of life the way it used to be."

Of course I'm sure that if he had his choice, he'd prefer to be able to retain his newfound ability to enjoy life and be cured of the cancer as well. But failing that, he's found a way to make the time he has remaining richer and more meaningful. My point is, we must find a way to realize how amazingly precious life itself is. Because if we could simply come to that realization, we'd lead the rest of our lives happy that we were just given the opportunity to live it.

Eliminate Your Two Biggest Problems

If you can learn how to restrict yourself to the present moment, you will have the ability to eliminate, at least for you, the two most debilitating problems that face the human race: guilt and fear.

You see, all of your failures and mistakes are in the past, and all of your fears have to do with the future. I would bet that nothing is happening right this moment to cause you any harm or distress. You're not failing or making any mistakes, and none of the things you fear have materialized. The only thing that connects the present moment with the guilt and regret of the past and with the fears of the unknown future are your *thoughts*. If you can find a way to disconnect from those thoughts, you will find yourself in a safe, secure, wonderfully carefree moment, suspended in time. All you have to do to be totally free is...be here now.

When I go off out into the woods by my home and sit down under a magnificent old oak tree, and put myself totally in the moment, the feeling of peace, security, and serenity is literally indescribable. I am, for those moments, completely free from the tyranny of negative thoughts and the hollow promises of my desires. And when I purposely create that state of mind, I carve out a little piece of life just for me. It's one of the biggest favors I can do for myself.

Centering

To help you reach a "be here now" appreciation, let me suggest that you get acquainted with the practice of centering. Centering is a mini-meditation you can conduct even during the middle of a busy day. It's an opportunity to temporarily stop your external life and put your higher self back in charge.

Anytime your external life becomes more important to you than your internal one, the emotional pull of your Lower Self takes over and begins to affect your behavior. You might be getting angry at someone at work, or maybe you're starting to feel overwhelmed with anxiety because you have to make an important presentation. Or it could be that you're feeling helpless or stressed out because you're being pressured and rushed to get something done. Anytime something like this happens, when you feel your negative emotions gaining the upper hand, you should realize that not only is your quality of life being disturbed, but these kinds of emotional conditions are also likely to keep you from making good decisions and functioning in an efficient and productive way. Anytime this happens, declare a time out...and get centered.

The first step is to get alone. This might be as easy as closing the door to your office or finding another private place for a few minutes. You could even get in your car, close the door, and use your vehicle as a place for centering.

Once you get quiet and still, close your eyes, take some deep breaths, and relax. Make everything slow down. Then remind yourself of your core beliefs. Remember that you are a spiritual being having a human experience. That life is a school to be learned from. That your serenity, inner peace, and ability to savor each moment are the keys to your happiness.

Then, once you've reminded yourself of the reality you've chosen to live in, refuse to think any thought that doesn't concern itself with what's going on right here...right now. Spend five minutes totally in the present moment, not allowing yourself to think about the past or the future or what's going on back at work. Centering provides you with an opportunity to gain control of your emotions and put everything back in its proper perspective. It's a time set aside especially for you to remind yourself what your life is really all about.

Then, after your little break from the world, take your newly acquired calmness and serenity back to your outward life. After all, there's no question that one of your lives is going to influence the other. You'll either be able to bring the peace of your internal life into your daily physical reality, or you will inadvertently allow the stress and pressure from the outside world to pollute your internal life. The choice, of course, is yours. But whatever you choose...choose it now, because now is all there is.

Life Lesson 13

Gratitude Makes the Best Attitude

It's really strange how and where life teaches us its lessons. This one I learned in a phone booth. I was taking a little trip by car a few years ago when I remembered that I needed to make a phone call. After a while I pulled over at a gas station on the side of a highway where I had finally spotted a phone booth. As I walked over to it, I retrieved the number from my wallet and then, as I made the call, laid the wallet on a little shelf there beside the phone.

To tell you the truth, I don't even remember what the call was about, but I must have been real proud of whatever negotiations took place that morning because when I was finished with the call I just walked back out to my car and got back on the road. I had been traveling again for about ten minutes when it hit me.

You know that feeling that grabs your gut when you realize you've done something really stupid....like realizing in the second that the door slams shut that you've left your keys inside?

Well, I realized in a flash that I had left my wallet back in that phone booth. My heart began to pound, and then, as the depth of my stupidity sunk in, I started calling myself names. I just couldn't believe I'd been so dumb.

I just knew my wallet was gone. The traffic is very heavy on that little road and that was the only phone booth within 50 miles—I know because I drove 50 miles looking for it! But with a tiny glimmer of hope, I turned the car around and raced back to that phone booth. I slid my car up to the phone booth, jumped out, ran over, and to my absolute amazement and utter delight, found my wallet there, apparently untouched.

I was so happy! I'm looking through my wallet just to make sure everything is still there. And, sure enough, there are all my credit cards—I don't have to go through the hassle of calling all of those companies to cancel them. I still have my driver's license—I don't have to go down to the Motor Vehicle Department and stand in line for four hours to get a duplicate. There are the irreplaceable pictures of my two daughters. And, of course, all of my cash is still right there in the wallet. By this point I am standing in that phone booth with a huge grin on my face saying: "Yes! Thank you, thank you! I am so happy!"

Then I think, "Wait a minute...I had all this stuff in my wallet this morning. *I wonder why I wasn't all this happy about it then?*"

About then I got the strangest feeling that there was a lesson here somewhere...if I could just figure out what it was.

Then there was the one time in my life that I checked into a hospital. It turned out that I needed major surgery. Without going into the details of that operation, let me just say that as a result of that hospital stay, I was unable to sit down for about a month. Now, I could stand up and I could lie down, but I couldn't sit. Let me tell you a valuable lesson I learned from that experience: *Sitting down is one of the most wonderful blessings of this life!* I no longer need a Mercedes Benz to be happy. Just let me sit down every now and then and I can find a way to be happy.

Are you understanding what I'm saying? Through these two experiences and some others that delivered the same message, I began to get the idea that gratitude could be my greatest ally in creating my own happiness.

You know, we don't take the time to remember to be thankful for the good things in our lives, especially if we're ambitious and have set ourselves a lot of lofty goals to reach. We spend most of our time concentrating on what we want but don't yet have. And when we take our hopes for the future to the extreme and live our lives for them, we spend our time wasting whatever we do have.

I had an interesting experience on an airplane not too long ago. As a public speaker I fly a lot, and for some reason, at the beginning of my career, I formed a preference for aisle seats. I

144

guess I favor them because they allow you to have at least one side of you that isn't packed in, shoulder to shoulder, with all those other people.

But on this flight, there were no aisle seats left, and so I ended up sitting by a window for the first time in years.

As I sat there looking out over the wing while the rest of the passengers were boarding, I decided, for some reason, to play a little game. I pretended that I was a pioneer from a couple of hundred years ago. I imagined that I had been standing out beside my wagon with my buckskins on, when some way-out, fancy-dressed dude came up to me and told me that he was from the future and that he had a machine that would take people up into the air. Well, of course I was skeptical, but I was also very curious and so I followed him to this strange-looking, very shiny contraption. I went inside, sat down by a window, and, hanging on to my imaginary identity, waited to see what was going to happen.

The huge machine moved out onto a field and then, to my absolute shock and amazement, the thing began to move *very* fast and then *lifted up into the air!*

My nose stayed jammed against the window as I watched everything on the ground get smaller and smaller as we continued to rise. Then, all of the sudden, I couldn't see anything but a solid white fog out the window and I reasoned that we must be *inside* a cloud! Then we popped out on top of the cloud and I looked down on it...imagine *looking down on a cloud!* Wow, what a magnificent sight that was!

Now, if that had actually happened to a pioneer two hundred years ago, it would have been the biggest day of his life. He would have told everyone he met from then on about the time he went above the clouds and looked down at the top of them.

But, you know, those clouds haven't changed a bit in the last two centuries. He wouldn't have seen anything I didn't see. But he'd have been awed by the experience—one that I just take for granted most of the time. We miss so much of life when we get used to the wonders of it and start taking them for granted. If we get something, we become familiar with it, and as soon as that happens, we start taking it for granted and stop appreciating it. Then, of course, we shift our focus to something we *don't* have. Indeed, our natural tendency is to concentrate on the negative things we need to fix and to forget about the things we have going for us—the things that make our lives pleasurable and worthwhile. And then we just can't figure out why we aren't happy.

The Creative Use of Gratitude

Well, I made myself a promise standing in that phone booth that day. I vowed that every morning for the rest of my life, as soon as I woke up, I'd spend a few minutes kind of mentally looking through my wallet...taking note of all the things I have to be thankful for.

One of our biggest challenges in life is to learn how to put ourselves into a desired state of mind. Of course the state of mind we wish for more than any other is happiness—and gratitude and happiness are almost synonymous. It's almost impossible to spend some time remembering what you have to be thankful for without putting yourself in a better mood.

You see, each morning when I fulfill that promise to myself, I take myself back to the state of mind I was in when I met the people I love and began the relationships with them that are so important to me. I also go back to the same state of mind I was in when I initially received all my wonderful material things. And since I still have most of them, and since I still have my loved ones, I choose to remain thankful for them, rather than forgetting about them and immediately drifting back into an unhappy frame of mind by concentrating on the things I don't have.

So let me suggest that the most important thing you can do at the beginning of each day is to set your mood for that day. Setting aside some time every morning to put yourself in the right state of mind for the day is a great habit to get into. Ed Foreman has told hundreds of thousands of people in audiences all across the country that it is up to them, each morning, to

146

choose what kind of day they're going to have. And that's really true—we *do* decide. *You* will make each day of your life a good day or a bad day—even if you don't know you can! And you can start each day off in the right direction by purposely spending some time reflecting on all of the things you have to be thankful for.

Sometimes when I go outside and sit down under my favorite old oak tree, I practice what I call "*the celebration of the absence of adversity.*" It works like this. I just think of some terrible thing that could be happening to me....that isn't. Then I think, "Wow, I'm sure glad I'm not having to go through that!" And, you know, the bigger the tragedy I can conjure up, the happier I get! Why do we have to wait until some tragedy really does come upon us before we can realize how happy we *should* have been before it happened?

After all, once I had been in that hospital for a while, it got much easier for me to see what was important and what wasn't. I spent a couple of weeks in such misery that I realigned most of my priorities. All of a sudden just being free from pain was more important than anything else in my life. All I wanted was chance to be left alone, and not to hurt. It wasn't important to me any longer that I have a lot of exciting, wonderful things happening to me. I was ready to be ecstatically happy if I could just get to a point where *nothing* was happening to me.

But we forget these valuable lessons that life teaches us unless we purposely make it a point to remember them. You wouldn't believe how often I think back to the time I was lying in that hospital bed and my total life's ambition was not to hurt. You see, I now use that memory to make today's petty complaints lose their importance.

So, understanding that your day will start however you decide to start it, spend some time counting your blessings, realizing how well off you are, remembering all the things you have going for you—and get happy.

How to Play Disturb The Peace

I've had people tell me that it makes sense to them to spend time forming an attitude of gratitude each morning. They were certain they could master starting their day off right, in a great mood. But then they asked, "With all the negative people we have to deal with throughout the day, how can we possibly *stay* in that positive, grateful frame of mind?" Well, it's much easier than you would think. In fact, I dreamed up a little piece of thought management that I call "playing Disturb the Peace" to address that very problem. Let me explain it to you by telling you how it came about.

As you can imagine, maintaining a good attitude while living in prison is somewhat of a challenge for an inmate. And so, a few years ago, I devised a game I could play with an inmate during my prison seminars that would show everyone how easy it is to hang on to a positive frame of mind if you know how.

I would first explain to them how to take a few moments each morning to get themselves into a good mood for the day. Then I would announce that we were going to play a game called Disturb the Peace. Here's how it worked. I would take a chair up to the front of the room and place it so that it was facing the audience. Then I would select one of the guys attending the session and have him come up front and sit in the chair. I would explain to him that he and I were opponents in this game and then I would explain how the game works.

I'd tell him that he would have a couple of minutes to close his eyes and think back on some special occasion in his life and that he should purposely use that pleasant memory to get himself in a good mood. His first assignment, then, is simple—get happy and peaceful. Now as soon as I see that pleasant look come to his face, I start the game by setting a timer for ten minutes. I explain that the object of the game for him is to stay in his good mood. If, when the bell rings at the end of that ten minute period, he's still happy and peaceful...he wins the game.

Then I tell him, "But here's the catch: I'm your opponent and I didn't name this game Disturb the Peace for nothing. You see, for the next ten minutes, while you try to maintain your composure and stay in a good mood, I'm going to do everything I can to disturb your peace. I'm going to do my best to get you uptight, frustrated, and just plain old mad at me. And if I do, I win the game."

Now, I always give him a couple of hints on how to play the game because, unlike me, he's never played it before. I tell him that the real key to winning is to make his number one priority for the next ten minutes his peace of mind. I warn him that he cannot let anyone or anything become more important to him than his good mood, because if he does, I'm going to get him. The minute he allows me or what I'm saying to become more important than his happiness, it will be over. He will have voluntarily thrown in the towel.

The second thing I tell my opponent is that I am at a major disadvantage. Because, you see, his peace is *inside* him and I, of course, have to stay *outside* of him. He's the only one in there, so if his peace gets disturbed, he'll have to be the one who disturbs it. The only thing I can try to do is sucker him into disturbing his *own* peace. And so we begin the game with the understanding that he may end up the loser, but I won't have beaten him—he will have done that to himself.

Do you want to hear something really interesting? In all the times I've played Disturb the Peace, I have never once won that game. In fact, it would go pretty much the same way every time. My opponent would sit in that chair at the front of the room with his arms folded and a big grin on his face, while I went around the room hurling insults at him. And I was vicious. I'd call him every name I could think of, but every time I did, his grin would just get bigger! Every one of them had a great time playing my game!

Now let's stop and review this situation for just a moment. This man is a criminal! In the past, he hasn't exercised enough self control to even keep his behavior within the bounds of being legal. I have even (unknowingly!) played this game with a murderer....a guy who killed two people in a fit of rage. Yet here he is, in front of all his macho prison buddies, with some

149

seminar pantywaist calling him all kinds of names, and he's unaffected—he's in complete control! How? Why?

Because he's trying to win the stupid little game we're playing. You see, he's always *had* the ability to control himself—he just never saw the need! Do you remember I told you that whether you win or lose in life usually depends on how you define the victory? Well, the only thing that's happened to this man is that—for ten minutes—we redefined his victory. You see, up until that point, the way he "won" in that kind of situation was to show his manhood by punching the offending person in the mouth. Of course, the corrections officers would then immediately appear and haul him off to solitary for a month or so. Then there would be a hearing and, as a result, his sentence would be extended for another six months or a year. Some victory, huh?

But for the ten minutes he played my game, we redefined the victory for him, and when we did, we changed his path of least resistance. After all, behavior is just a matter of what's important to us, and while he was playing Disturb the Peace he remembered my instructions and made his happiness more important than what I was saying to him. Once he understood that the way to win was to keep his cool, suddenly he had the ability to do it.

And so all you have to do to maintain a happy state of mind—no matter what happens to you during your day—is attain and then maintain an attitude of gratitude.

If happiness is your number one goal, then make your priorities reflect that importance. Begin training yourself to operate with the mind set that your happiness is more important than anything that could happen to you. Staying in a positive frame of mind should be more important to you than getting all annoyed because your flight just got canceled. It ought to be more important than the fact that you didn't land the big deal, or get that promotion. And remaining happy certainly ought to be more important than anything anyone might say to you.

In fact, people who upset you by saying petty, insulting things aren't really saying what you think you hear them say.

Let me translate their comments for you. When someone comes up and says something negative or demeaning to you, what he's really saying is, "Excuse me, but I was wondering if I could get you to *ruin your day for me?* You see, I'm a very miserable person and I've learned that if I say the right thing to you, you'll get all upset and then *we can be miserable together for the rest of the day!*"

Now, you can react with anger and comply with this guy's wishes if you want to, but if you'll think about it for a moment, I think you'll realize that he's simply not that important to you. Why would you want to let someone take from you that which you desire more than anything else in life...your happiness?

But what if they're *really* ugly and mean? What if they get real nasty and say horrible things to you? Then you must bring out the really big ammunition. You have to hit them as hard as you can...with a double dose of *understanding!* Then you'll probably want to follow that up with a swift round of *forgiveness.* And if they're bad enough you may even be forced to *choose to love them.*

In the school of life every person you meet is a teacher...and I mean *every* person. In fact, often it's the people who know the least who unwittingly give us the opportunity to learn the most. They teach us compassion, forbearance, forgiveness, and love. And those, of course, are the most important lessons in the curriculum of the school we call life.

Live According to Your Own Inward Agenda

Here's how I make this attitude of gratitude a part of my daily life. As you've learned, first I set aside some time *every* morning for getting myself in a happy, peaceful state of mind. This attitude-setting time includes a review of all the things that are happening right in my life so I can fill my mind with gratitude. The rest of the time is made up of a meditation session and reading some uplifting inspirational literature. By the time I leave the house each morning, I'm in a great mood. Then it's time to implement part two of my plan.

I purposely decide that my happiness is more important than anything that might happen to me during that day. Now I know this sounds pretty simple, but it is so powerful! Give it a try. Make this a part of your daily thought management routine. All you have to do—just like the inmates who won the game of Disturb the Peace—is to remember your priorities, and not only will you enjoy your day more, you'll be more efficient and productive. After all, you can certainly deal with any problem that might come your way in a more effective manner if you've maintained your peace of mind.

Oh, and let me tell you one more thing about playing Disturb the Peace. Each time I'd play that game in a prison, I would ask the victorious inmate one question when he goes back to his chair. I have that same question for you. "What's the difference between playing Disturb the Peace for ten minutes with me here today...and playing it all day, every day, for the rest of your life?"

There is only one difference. When you play in real life, your opponents don't know they're playing the game. Now, I don't think I have to tell you that it's a lot easier to win a game when your opponent doesn't even *know* he's playing! So live each day according to your own inward agenda. Why get pulled into what other people are doing and adopt their priorities? If you know how to get happy with the creative use of gratitude, and how to make that attitude more important than anything that might happen outside you, you'll become one of the small number of people who decide how much they're going to enjoy life, and then happily implement that decision.

Try it tomorrow. Oh, sure, there's a good chance something will happen that will overpower your resolve, but that's only because you'll be new at playing the game. With each additional day you play Disturb the Peace, you'll get better at it. And I promise that soon you'll be amazed at how much difference it can make, and how much better you'll be able to handle things as a result of just understanding how much power there is in an attitude built out of gratitude.

Life Lesson 14

Life Is a School

Did you ever notice that some people seem to live totally carefree lives, while others are always mired in some kind of adversity? I have. In fact, for years it was a constant source of wonderment for me. I just couldn't figure out what the big difference was. Are some people just luckier than others? Or have they acquired some sort of unique life skill? Well, there's one thing that's for sure: Some people sure do have a lot easier time of it than others.

In the last few years I've begun to understand that life, in many ways, is like a game. We're all playing the same game and, believe it or not, the rules are identical for everybody. The main reason that some folks win and others always seem to find themselves on the losing end is that some people have a better understanding of those rules and can play the game better than others.

When we enter this life, it's as if we were born in the middle of a gigantic playing field. Of course at first we don't know it's a playing field because we can't see very much of it. We don't even know there's a game going on, much less how to win it. And we can only play the game of life to the degree that we can see it. In fact, it's all a matter of light. The more light we have, the better we understand the game.

Imagine, if you will, that you suddenly find yourself standing in the center of a basketball court—except you don't know it's a basketball court because most of it is shrouded in darkness and you can't see further than your hand. A buzzer sounds and you begin to hear the sounds of a game; a ball bouncing, people cheering, shoes screeching as they grip the floor. The problem is, you are expected to play—and even try to *win*—this game! Would the fact that you don't have the foggiest idea what's going on around you hinder your efforts to play? Without question.

The only way to gain the ability to win this game is to find out more about it—to increase your awareness of the playing area and the rules that govern it. And you're not going to do that until you find a way to turn some more lights on. Your first goal, then, is to find some light switches and get the court illuminated so you can better distinguish your opponents, and your teammates, and get some idea of how points are scored.

Living your life isn't a great deal different from knowing how to play a game. Your ability to live life successfully will be directly dependent upon how aware you can become of what life is about.

Because of my prison work I've had the privilege of getting to know Harry Singleterry, Jr., Secretary of the Department of Corrections for the state of Florida. He's a big, imposing man with a heart that I suspect is even bigger. One time Harry was telling me about how he played checkers with his grandfather when he was a kid. He said when he was first learning the game, as hard as he tried, he always lost. There were times that he would move one of his checkers, sometimes very early in the game, and his grandfather would look at him and say, "You're through."

And Harry would respond, "What do you mean, 'I'm through? I just started!"

And then his grandfather would say, "No, son, it's all over. We may as well start another game...you've lost this one."

One day, in exasperation, Harry asked his granddad how he always managed to win.

The old man said: "You lose these games because you can only see your next play; you're dealing with just one move at a time. But when I look at the board, I see the next ten or twelve moves. Every time you move one of those checkers, you set up a chain of events and I can see far enough ahead to know what's going to happen to you, although you don't see any of it coming."

154

You see, Harry Singleterry's grandfather had learned enough about the game to see much more of what was going on than his inexperienced opponent. Harry could barely figure out what his next *move* should be, and he had no idea of what ramifications that move would bring about in the future. But the old man saw things that Harry couldn't possibly see. More of the game was illuminated for him, and so at that point, winning a game of checkers became almost effortless.

We're Here to Find the Light

Our job is to find the light switches and turn them on so we can see what's really going on here. That's what "enlightenment" means. It's increasing our awareness so we can see things more clearly. Wisdom, awareness, enlightenment—those are our goals. They are what we're here to obtain. And as soon as we learn enough of life's lessons to be able to judge the *extended* effects of the things we think, say, and do, we will be able to make our lives as "lucky" as the lives of those people who seem to always end up on top.

There are two kinds of students in every school: those who realize what they are there for and those who don't. You can always recognize a member of the former group. They're the ones who are always asking questions. They listen more than they talk. They're pliable, always willing to change their thinking to accommodate a greater truth. A kid who takes his role of student seriously and makes a conscious effort to be a good one is always in a learning mode. After all, it's his *job.*

And then there are the kids in every school who are too smart to learn anything. They already know it all. They don't want to listen, they want to talk. Unfortunately, the most dependable symptom of ignorance is an illusion of knowledge. People who think they know everything don't know much of anything in reality. It's when they gain enough light to realize they don't know a lot that they're starting to figure things out.

We all know that the student who has the attitude that he or she doesn't have enough knowledge will be the one to benefit

155

most from the learning process. That's exactly what we ourselves have to become: someone who realizes that, as students, our main function is to learn. Oh, life has the ability to teach us even if we don't want to learn, but that's a much tougher way to go about it. In fact, I'm convinced that's why many of us experience so many adversities in life. Those adversities are there to teach us the lessons we couldn't learn any other way.

I tell the prison inmates I lecture to that life is not their enemy...it's their teacher. If life appears to be an adversary, it's probably because they're stuck on a lesson. And then, like a loving parent, life is left with no choice but to kick them a little harder each time it presents the lesson, in an attempt to get their attention so they can learn, grow, and become enlightened enough to lead a more successful life.

How This School Works

I have a lot of people who ask me: "If this is a school, how does it work? What am I supposed to do? How will I know if I'm doing it right?" Well, those are very good questions, and I'm happy to tell you that the answers are very simple and easy to understand. You see, you came here with all the equipment necessary to attend this grand school successfully. There are really only three things you need to remember in order to be an honor student in the school of life.

1. Always Be Looking for the Next Lesson

The first step is to realize that you are attending a school and that your primary function is to learn life's lessons as they are presented to you. Most people don't like the idea that they're students of the school of life because, you see, this school doesn't teach you what's wrong with other people. It offers a lifelong course in how to correct *your* misconceptions and make *you* a better person.

The most vehement opponent of the learning process is our sense of self-importance. A lot of people find it almost impossible to operate with an attitude that reflects the idea that they're far from perfect and have a lot to learn. Our pride, our ego, doesn't like the idea that we're going around looking for direction. That mind-set is very uncomfortable for those of us who feel a great need for other people to look up to us and admire us. Indeed, the Lower Selfs natural tendency is to adopt an attitude of superior knowledge. Our Lower Self isn't in the least bit interested in taking admonishment or correction. That's why it's so hard to adopt an attitude of humility, but that's exactly what's necessary in order for us to have an attitude that is conducive to learning.

Every morning we should get up with the understanding that there are important things to learn that we don't know about yet. Unless we are willing to correct our mistakes and revise our thinking and way of living, we're going to continue to lead the same kind of life we've led up until now. There's an old saying, "If you keep on doing what you've always done, you're gonna keep on getting what you always got"—and that's really very true!

So first we must adopt an attitude of constantly looking for more light, and then we need to be willing to change ourselves in order to accommodate each new truth as we discover it.

With that attitude, then, purposely begin a lifelong search for your next lesson. You see, we each have our own individual curriculum. This is a very personalized school, and although we are exposed to countless lessons all day, every day, some major lessons are presented to us in a way that uniquely speaks to *us* and to *our* needs. But how do you know when life is presenting a major lesson to you? You'll know...believe me, you'll know. All you have to do is *look for the next lesson,* and stay open to the idea that some person, some event, some occurrence in your life will come along expressly for the purpose of teaching you a lesson that will turn on a light or two.

Anytime something significant happens to you—whether it's good or bad, or somewhere in between—ask yourself: "Is this

157

my next lesson? Is there something I'm supposed to learn from this?" It's impossible for you to stay in this frame of mind without readily discovering the multitude of lessons life has to offer you. My promise to you is that if you will begin looking for your next lesson, you will find it. And when you do, you'll know it.

A few years ago I became convinced, through a series of events, that life was trying to teach me a major lesson about anger. Oh, I can't tell you exactly how I initially came across the idea that it was my next lesson, but there were several things that eventually led me to that conclusion, including some intuitive "feelings" as the lesson began to unfold for me. What I can tell you about, though, are the two events that finally convinced me. I remember them very well.

One day as I was watching a news story on television, I saw a little seven-or-eight-year-old boy who was throwing a classic temper tantrum in full view of the camera. I'm sure he got to see it on television later, and when he did, he must have been terribly embarrassed by how ridiculous he looked. His face was distorted and he was totally out of control. No one who witnessed that scene would have envied or admired that little boy. As I watched I said to myself, "I hope I never even approach that attitude. I can't think of a way to make myself any uglier."

The very next day, I was out on my morning run when a pickup truck passed by me and then apparently ran over something because one of its tires quickly went flat. After the driver pulled over to the curb to see what was wrong, he let go of a vile string of obscenities at the top of his lungs. Then he slammed the door on his truck so hard that I thought the window would break. He capped off this display of enlightenment and self-discipline by kicking the fender of that old truck as hard as he possibly could. His face was beet red and the veins in his neck were bulging. He was totally out of control and completely miserable. I just can't adequately describe to you how stupid he looked.

And that's when it clicked: "Life is giving me a message about anger—it's ugly, it's unnecessary, and it destroys the inner peace for everyone who allows it to take hold." I decided that day that I have absolutely no need for anger. It may have served men well in some earlier stage of human development—maybe it was invaluable back in the Stone Age—but I just can't, for the life of me, find a good use for anger in my life today. It makes us say things we later regret. It disturbs our peace. And worst of all, it does a lot of damage to relationships when we unthinkingly lash out at a loved one.

2. Put It into Practice

Okay, step two. Once you know what the lesson is, get busy and become a proactive student. Make an effort to participate in the learning process and adopt the lesson.

You see, once life decides to present you with your next lesson, that lesson isn't going to go away just because you can't see it or don't care to adopt it. And you have a choice about how, where, and how fast you learn and adopt each of the lessons in your life. Doing so won't always be easy; there will be times you'll have to swallow some pride before you can admit that the way you understood things was wrong. But as soon as you make the changes necessary to accommodate each new lesson and put your old misconceptions behind you, you will have grown. And we need that growth to give our lives meaning and purpose.

Let me tell you what I did with my lesson on anger. First, I thought about it...a lot. I knew that suppressing my anger wasn't healthy to do, that I had to learn to respond in a totally different way to those things that I had, in the past, met with wrath. I decided that what I needed to do was mix a healthy dose of understanding into the situations that had always made me mad. I came to believe that if I gained a deep enough understanding of *why* something happened, it would diffuse my tendency toward anger.

And so, using conscious manual override, I spent some time readjusting my responses to situations that had traditionally upset me. Then when something negative happened, I would analyze it—not in terms of why I didn't like it and what it was doing to me emotionally, but in terms of *why* it happened. I'd ask myself, "What's the real reason for this event?" And you know, every time I did, I would remember a very insightful quote from Longfellow: "If we could read the secret history of our enemies, we should find in each man's life sorrow and suffering enough to disarm all hostility." That's great advice, and it sure works for me.

I spent a lot of energy and effort retraining my emotional response to the people and events that used to make my blood boil and ruin the rest of my day. You see, it doesn't do you any good to learn a Life Lesson if you don't find a way to use it, implement it, and make it a part of your life. My friend Mark Haroldsen, author of <u>Awakening The Financial Genius Inside You</u>, often says, "To know and not to do, is not to know." What he means is, it's not enough just to learn something. You must put it into practice. Only then does it serve you.

3. Then....Get Ready for the Test!

Well, what did you expect? I told you life was a school. When did you ever attend a school without having to take a test? I'll promise you that this life is *full* of tests to help you measure how far you've come and how effectively you've been able to implement the lessons you've learned.

The problem is, they don't look like tests. They look more like...some turkey out on the freeway. There I'd be, driving along, halfway to winning the war I had declared on my anger, when all of the sudden some idiot changes four lanes at once, almost knocks my front fender off as he cuts in just ahead of me, and *then blames me for his terrible driving!*

Now, there he is, up in front of me, letting me know what he thinks of me by waving his fist in the air. In fact, as I look closer, I do believe he even has the optional attachment extended!

Well, he can't do that! Did you see what he did? It just burns me up. If there's anything I can't stand it's somebody who does something wrong and then, rather than admit it, blames *me* for it!

So I step on the gas and scoot up alongside him, roll down my window, and take the sweet revenge that can only come from chewing somebody out that really needs it.

And then it hits me like a bucket of cold water. I just flunked a test! You see, I forgot, just for that moment, that life is a school and that I'm right in the middle of a class in Anger 101. I guess I thought we had suspended school for a minute— long enough for me to straighten this guy out. Wrong. He was *a plant!* He was there so I could see if I had really learned that lesson or if I was just performing mental gymnastics with it. And what did I get on the test? An "F." So now I am forced to remind myself one more time that everything happens for a reason, including this little freeway incident.

The good news is, *life is willing to give you that lesson again!* In fact, it will give us that test over and over...countless times, until we finally pass it. The reason a lot of people never seem to make any progress in life is that they never learn life's lessons well enough to pass the tests. And until you pass the test (or tests) on your present lesson, you can't move on to the next one.

After I fail a test, my next course of action is obvious. I must get back in the learning mode (step two) and try again until I get it right.

Now let me give you a little piece of advice on how to pass life's tests. Are you ready? Here it comes...*be looking for the test!* Pretty simple, huh? You see, if I had realized the guy in the car on the freeway was a test, I would have handled it in a much different way. But, instead, I forgot I was in school! Big mistake.

To successfully use the advice I've just given you, imagine that a higher-up at work has just enough authority to think he

161

can chew you out for something, and decides to do so. He strides into your work space and starts saying some things to you that shouldn't be said to anyone. Now, of course, when this happens, your familiar internal red light starts to blink. Your eyes narrow and your hands automatically start to clench into fists. But then, just before you explode, you realize what's really happening—just like those folks used to on that old television show <u>Candid Camera</u>. You say to yourself: "Wait a minute. This isn't some middle management simpleton chewing me out...*this is a test!* It's a test of my new policy on anger. Now, I've got to admit it almost fooled me this time, but I'm back in charge, and I remember that it's more important to pass this test and advance on to the next lesson than it is to chew this creep—er, gentleman—out."

Then, put the biggest grin you can find on your face, and staring him straight in the eye say: "Thank you for pointing all this out to me. I want you to know that I appreciate your help. Now, since you've identified the problem, rest assured that I'll take care of it. Don't worry another moment about it. Now go have yourself a *gooood day!*"

Now, he *will* leave, disarmed by your magnanimous attitude and receptive nature. Best of all he be taking that black cloud with him because he couldn't get you to buy into it. And you'll be left standing there knowing that not only did your preserve your inner peace, you passed another test...and grew some. *And that's what you're here for.*

Learn in Abundance

Well, that's how you attend the school of life. Just remember, *those who are looking for knowledge always find it.* And when they do, with just a little effort and some momentary discomfort, they can grow and benefit from that knowledge.

Oh, I have one more little piece of advice. Vow daily to be the kind of person who can grow, learn, and mature...in abundance. You see, if you insist upon being backed against a wall before you can learn from the experiences life offers you,

162

you'll spend most of your time backed against one. But if you can manage to be one of the few people who can grow and mature spiritually when things are going good, you'll find yourself living a life full of prosperity. You see, I honestly believe that life loves us. It's our friend...our teacher. Its goal is to assist us in our quest for knowledge, and I'm convinced it would rather bless us than punish us. After all, isn't that the way we feel about our children? The only reason we don't give them more of the things they want is that they would be worse off for it.

Wouldn't it be wonderful if your children could grow and mature while getting everything they wanted? But if you've been a parent for more than fifteen minutes, you know that covering a child up in abundance won't benefit him, it will spoil him. As a result, we learned a long time ago that you just can't give your children everything they want because they can't find a way to grow when things are going well. Unfortunately, they make their best progress toward maturity when they have to suffer for their mistakes. But I don't think that's a written law. Why wouldn't it be possible for a child to be smart enough to figure out that if he was determined to grow and stay in line when things were going good, his parents wouldn't have any reason to make things bad for him?

I remember I used to beg my daughters to "please let me be nice to you." And they knew what I meant. I was really saying, "police yourselves so I won't have to."

That's exactly what I'm telling you we need to do if we want life to treat us to the things we'd like to have. If you want life to bless to you then remove all of its reasons not to. Become a person who can grow, develop, and mature in abundance. Oh, obviously, there'll still be some lessons you'll have to learn the hard way, but why not eliminate all of them you can. You see, I'm convinced that the way to live a "lucky" life is to be a quick study.

163

Life Lesson 15

As You Do...You Do to You !

I've saved this lesson for last for a very good reason. It's the most important one I've ever learned. Unfortunately, though, it's also the most difficult to explain. So let me first give it to you in a nutshell, and then I'll try to fill in the blanks.

Are you listening carefully? Good. Then here it is. *You will never find lasting, genuine happiness unless and until you can find a way to set aside your own selfish interests and begin serving others.*

You see, self-centered, self-serving people are never happy. As strange as it may seem, selfish behavior is the biggest single barrier to happiness. It took me more than forty years to learn that lesson—forty years of very effectively grabbing everything I thought I wanted. After all, it just made sense to me that if I was trying to make myself happy, then that was the best way to accomplish it. But I couldn't have been further off base. Let me see if I can't give you some of the reasons why.

Pleasure Versus Fulfillment

The one thing that your Higher Self and your Lower Self agree on completely is what your most important goal should be. Both sides of you are seeking happiness. But your two personalities approach that goal in two totally different ways.

Our Lower Self takes the pleasure-based approach. It's a real simple way to create happiness, and we learned it when we were kids. You just find something that feels good and do it! And then, of course, you do it some more, and then you do it again. And then—well, you get the idea.

But there are some major problems with the Lower Selfs approach to happiness. Problems that become obvious when we become adults. In fact, when I speak in high schools, I ask the students if they've ever noticed that most adults don't seem to know how to be happy. Believe me, they *have.* And then I say something like, "Of course, you kids know how to be happy, don't you?" They always grin and nod.

Then I tell them something that they don't want to hear. I inform them that when we adults were their age, we knew how to be happy, too. It was easy back then. All you had to do was find the pleasure button and push it—a lot. Happiness was having a good time with our friends. It was going to the movies, or a ball game, or maybe out on a date with someone we really liked. But then I break it to them that, as the years go by, Mother Nature starts to play a trick on us. Little by little, as we gain in maturity, we realize, subconsciously at first, that a life dedicated to the pursuit of pleasure is a selfish, self-centered life...devoid of self respect.

When we reach that point in life, the fun starts to wear a little thin, but we can't figure out what to replace it with. And so we settle into lives of unhappiness, or at best mediocrity. The pleasure principle works great for children, but it just doesn't hack it for those of us who have turned a few lights on. Unfortunately though, that doesn't mean we stop trying to make it work. Our childhood training is hard to shake off. But, as adults, we eventually have to come to a clear understanding that *pleasure mistaken for happiness is life's most seductive illusion.*

And there are other reasons the pleasure-based approach to happiness doesn't work. Chief among them is the fact that when you dedicate your life to pleasure and spend most of your time in the pursuit of it, something very strange happens inside you.

It's a phenomenon that almost defies logic. Every time you satisfy a desire for pleasure, the desire just gets *bigger!* You can't satisfy a need for pleasure...with pleasure. The more you push that pleasure button, the more you want to push it. The classic illustration of this principle is the drug addict. The first time a person uses drugs, the pleasure is overwhelming. And the result is instantaneous—he just can't wait to get back into that euphoric state. Except next time it takes a little more of the drug and the effect is a little less. And the time after that, more yet, for even less. That's what the unfettered satisfaction of your desires does for you (or maybe I should say, does *to* you).

What we have here is a version of the law of supply and demand. When you allow yourself an abundance of pleasure it loses its value. And, as in the case of anything that's in oversupply, a life devoted to pleasure lessens the value of pleasure, eventually to the point of making it completely worthless.

On the other hand, people who are mature enough to realize this, and who have enough discipline to ration the pleasures they allow themselves, enjoy the ones they do indulge in much more. Because the pleasure is in short supply, it becomes more valuable.

So a life devoted to the pursuit of pleasure may look good on the drawing board, but it just won't fly.

The Other Side of The Equation

The Higher Self's approach to happiness is...fulfillment. Instead of seeking fun, thrills, and excitement to bring about happiness, the Higher Self pursues meaning, purpose, and fulfillment. The Lower Self, being externally based, delights in *things*. Of course the only way you can enjoy things is to have them, and the only way you can have them is to *take* them. But, you see, fulfillment only comes from *giving*. The higher part of us thrives on contribution and service to others. We have an inherent need to feel that we've done our part—to leave some evidence that we were here. And one thing is for sure: Your Higher Self's need for a worthwhile life will keep you from enjoying being a taker.

This is a lesson that so many grandmothers have mastered. You remember Grandmother, don't you? She was the one who always had your favorite cookies ready, no matter how late you got in that night. Remember how she used to knit your Christmas presents, although it must have been terribly painful to do such intricate work with her arthritic hands? And she didn't do it for a thank-you. If she even got one, it was muttered

167

without any conviction, when your parents told you to say it. No, she did it because she'd lived long enough and become wise enough to realize that the true joy in life is giving and serving. (Of course, the real joy in life is actually *loving*. But then, come to think of it, there isn't much of a distinguishable difference between giving, serving, and loving.)

Most of us get our first hint of how wonderful it is to give and serve when we become parents. It happens to you without your realizing it. All of a sudden there you are, on Christmas morning, and your three-year-old is opening her presents as fast as she possibly can. There's a look of sheer delight on her face. There's no question, this child is into *taking* and she's enjoying every minute of it! But did you notice that for maybe the first time in your life, you weren't interested in what you were getting? Your presents were lying there beside your chair, still unopened. Without realizing it, you had transcended the selfish need to receive. You were, instead, thrilled by the concept of giving.

That occurrence—one that each of us at some point experiences—is one of the biggest turning points in life. That's when we begin to understand that the biggest thrill available to us in this life is the joy and the love we feel when we put someone else's needs above ours. Think back to those Christmas mornings when your kids were little. See if you can recapture the memory of your mood, attitude, and state of mind when you were totally immersed in the role of giver and server, giving absolutely no thought to what *you* might receive. Because if you can capture that feeling, you'll realize that even today what you give away becomes your reward! The only things you can keep...are the things you give away.

I know a guy who loves to play basketball. He was a star in high school and he played his heart out in college, hoping to make it to the NBA. He didn't, but that didn't diminish his love for the game. He still plays in neighborhood basketball games with other men his age.

Now when this guy is out on the court, winning is everything to him. He's a taker. He needs to receive—to be the

168

victor. And, of course, when he wins, it gives him a lot of pleasure. He taunts his opponents and high-fives his teammates. But if you'd follow him home that evening, you'd find out that nowadays his biggest love in basketball is *losing*. You see, he has a seven-year-old son. Frankly, the boy isn't much of a basketball player, but he loves the game and he thoroughly enjoys playing with his dad because when he does, he usually wins. Oh, my friend makes it hard for his son to win—most of the time the kid just barely squeaks through. But when that little boy sinks the final basket and wins another game over his father, he's always delighted and full of pride and accomplishment. But let me tell you a little secret: He's not the happiest one on that driveway basketball court. His dad, while feigning displeasure at having lost again, is, in reality, full of joy because there isn't anything in life that makes him happier than seeing his son win and become more confident.

You see, when he's on the court with those other men, he's still competitive. He needs to win by causing someone else to lose. But when you put him in the arena of love, he transcends all of that. Can you imagine him playing the game as hard as he can so he can beat that little seven-year-old boy into the ground, and then maybe strut around with his finger up in the air chanting, "I'm number one, I'm number one!" That's ridiculous isn't it? Well, it's no more ridiculous than we are when we try to beat everyone else down in a valiant but totally ineffective effort to make ourselves feel good. It just won't work. It never has and it never will.

Spiritual Laws

I must admit to you that for years, when I heard the words, "It is more blessed to give than it is to receive," I misunderstood them...and dismissed them.

First of all, like so many of us, I totally separated spirituality from the rest of my life. You know how that works: You take all the "religious" stuff and put it over here in this pile. Then all the rest of your life goes over there in that one. And you never,

ever mix the two. I didn't realize that my spirituality was an intricate part of my everyday life. I thought that religious teachings had to do with some far off, after-you-die concept that I couldn't even understand, much less benefit from, in this life.

But after making that mistake for far too long, I came to the realization that those words are, in addition to whatever else you might think, words of great wisdom...to live *this* life by. They are the single most valuable key to happiness. You've probably also read the passage, "Whosoever shall seek to save his life shall lose it; and whoever shall lose his life shall preserve it" (Luke 17:33), and although that, too, is a spiritual principle, it is just as applicable on a practical day-to-day basis as we pursue our quest for happiness. The more we reach out to grab, the more we inadvertently rob ourselves of that which we reach for...no matter who we are, where we are, or what we've chosen to believe.

We all realize that there are laws that you just can't violate and remain successful. There are, of course, physical laws that we learn about early in our lives. If you make the mistake of jumping off the top of a tall building, the law of gravity will take its toll...*every time*. And we know there are mental or intellectual laws. Two plus two *always* equals four...no matter what.

But there are also spiritual laws that will not and cannot be avoided or denied. They can't be put off until Sunday morning and they are in effect 365 days a year— whether you're in a "spiritual" mood or not. The best understood of these laws is a concept shared by people around the world, no matter what their religious persuasion.

I told you earlier that in my study of the world's religions, I came across several of what I call "universal concepts"—things that *everybody* believes. And one of them stands head and shoulders above the others in its universal acceptance. We, in the Bible-reading Western world, call it the law of sowing and reaping, from the New Testament passage, "Whatsoever a man soweth, that shall he also reap"(Gal. 6:7). The Far Eastern religions know it as karma. The guys in prison usually call it

170

"what goes around comes around." In other words, you *get* what you *give*.

Now whether that makes any sense to you or not, let me point out that this principle has been embraced by *billions* of people around the world for *thousands* of years. Things just don't stay around that long unless they have some foundation in truth. I honestly believe that if we could get a clear understanding of how absolute, reliable, and consistent this basic spiritual law is, we would never even think another negative thought about another human being, much less take any adverse action toward anyone. You'll never get away from the fact that you will ultimately be the recipient of whatever you do to other people. I like to call this law "As you do...you do to you." This little rhyme sums it up perfectly (even if I do say so myself). When you go out into the world and plant your seeds, you are deciding what your harvest will be. The fact that you, in reality, give those seeds to others makes the concept a little harder to understand, but it doesn't invalidate the law or lessen any of its effects.

You see, liars get lied to. Cheaters get cheated. Thieves get stolen from. Givers receive, and takers...well, they get taken from. That's the law. Don't blame me, I didn't write it—Lord knows, I had a tough enough time even finding out about it!

But in case you have a more analytical mind and need logical reasons why you should be serving instead of taking, there are some of those, too.

Gaining Self-Respect—And The Respect of Others

I think we all know by now that self-respect is a necessary ingredient for happiness. But how do you gain enough self-respect to make a big difference in how you feel about yourself? Let me tell you the quickest, shortest route to self-respect I know of. It's really very simple: Recognize and then emulate that which we respect in other people.

Look at the truly great people throughout history...the ones we put on a pedestal, admire, and greatly respect. They all have something in common: a cause that they loved more than they loved themselves. Truly revered people, from Gandhi to Martin Luther King to Albert Schweitzer to Oskar Schindler to Mother Theresa, all have made sacrifices for their fellow human beings. We have always judged people based on how much they care. Everyone disrespects selfishness. We all look down on takers. We see them as immature and shallow. We view them as people who aren't enlightened and don't have much of an awareness of the deeper aspects of life.

Well, once we've acknowledged what we respect in other people, it's pretty simple to mix a healthy dose of that ingredient into our own lives. Finding a cause that you can care more for than you care for yourself and submerging yourself in that cause instantly builds an enormous amount of self-respect and puts you on an undeniable fast track to happiness.

Contributors Feel a Sense of Belonging

I have a lot of unpleasant memories about my failures as a student before I dropped out of school. But the one that's most vivid in my mind is a terrible feeling I had back then...of not belonging. I didn't feel a part of it all. That little, friendly farming town of Dimmitt, Texas, never seemed like *my* community.

It took a long time and the completion of a lot of life's lessons before I came to understand the real problem. You see, I was a taker. I was looking out for number one. And takers never really feel a sense of community because, deep down, on a subconscious level, they know that they're taking a free ride, enjoying the benefits of a society created and maintained by...contributors.

I didn't feel a part of my hometown community, simply because I had not earned my right to take part in it. I was a social leech—taking but never giving, always in selfish pursuit of what I wanted for *me.* Only contributors feel a sense of "community"—of belonging. When we start to pull our share of the load, we automatically gain the feeling that we have earned

172

the right to occupy our place in the universe. And ultimately, we gain a feeling of pride as a result of being a functioning, contributing part of the grand scheme of things.

I think that's why we have this compulsion to *possess* things. For most of my life I didn't have the ability to enjoy something unless it was mine. I might see a beautiful car going down the street, but instead of appreciating it and getting a good feeling from seeing it, all I would feel was the envy that I didn't own it. Why do we have to possess something before we can appreciate and enjoy it? I'll tell you why. Because we don't feel connected enough with the rest of humanity to enjoy what they have, and so we lack the ability to enjoy the fact that *they* have it.

Since I've learned about the joy of serving and have done my best to become a contributor, I have a whole new outlook on everything I see. You see that cloud up there? It's as much mine as it is anybody's. I have a love for the Gulf of Mexico and I enjoy the times I can take my boat out on that deep blue water as much as anything I do. I take pride in its crystal clear water and the foam crested waves as they roll up on the beaches. You see, the Gulf of Mexico is mine, or at least I'm a viable, active partner in its ownership because I'm living in a way that reflects my need to contribute to it, to feel an obligation toward it. And the same rings true with every aspect of life: Contributors feel a sense of pride and belonging. Takers, their arms filled with worthless possessions, look at life and wonder why they're not happy.

Giving Teaches Us to Love

I told you at the beginning of the chapter that this lesson was the most important one... and here's why. You see, among the lessons life has to offer is love. Love does not come naturally to us. It has to be learned. For some reason women seem to have an easier time learning it than men do, but I'm convinced that none of us arrive here with the capacity for genuine love. Real

173

love is a *choice*—it knows no boundaries and it isn't conditional upon anything.

I gave a speech once to an annual banquet of the Salvation Army. Just before I spoke, the group was addressed by one of their national leaders. He said, "It is our mission *to love the unlovable.*" Wow, now there's a calling! You see, we don't have a problem displaying what passes for love toward the pretty people, or the successful ones. But we have to *learn* to love the filthy, smelly wino sleeping in Grand Central Station. And you'll never get out of life all it has to offer until you do. Your ability to be happy will always be directly proportional to your capacity to love. You see, love *is* happiness. I'm not saying *being* loved—Elvis Presley was loved by virtually the entire world, and still was terribly unhappy—but *feeling* love. If you're looking for happiness you'll never find a happier, more joyful state of mind than the act of loving. Look at the joy your children bring you: It's because you've learned to love them...unconditionally.

Now here's the important part—please pay careful attention. You *learn* to love by serving and giving to others. You see, when it comes to love, we have cause and effect transposed. The popular idea is, as soon as I love you I'll begin doing things for you. But that's backwards. It's when you begin to serve and give to others that you gain the capacity for loving them. The more you do for others, the more you'll care about them. And the more people you help, the larger that joyful feeling will grow.

Think back to the last time that you did something totally unselfish for another person. You felt better about yourself afterwards, didn't you? But, more important, I would bet that you also gained a new and deeper feeling of caring for that person. That's the way it works.

Please remember, you'll never be able to *take* your way to fulfillment. And without meaning, purpose, and fulfillment, you can't be happy. The ultimate answer is to grow and mature so that one day you can feel toward the entire human race—all of us, no matter what color, religion, nationality, or status in life—

174

the way you feel about your own little kids on Christmas morning. And when that happens...well, let's just say that will be your graduation day.

About the Author

He's been called "America's greatest salesman" by Morley Safer and profiled by *Newsweek* and *The Wall Street Journal*. Joe Land overcame his beginnings as a grammer school dropout to become a self-made millionaire. But it wasn't until he retired that he discovered "Real Success." Now he helps everyone discover the keys to fulfillment and happiness.

Joe Land has made millions in real estate, seminars, and direct television marketing. He conducts seminars to sellout audiences throughout the country. He lives near Tallahassee, Florida.